MW01630072

ANNE DE BERGH

JOYCE BRIAND

Traduction de REGAN KRAMER

archives & culture

© 2016, Archives & Culture, 26 bis rue Paul-Barruel, 75015 Paris - www.archivesetculture.fr
ISBN : 978-2-911665-98-1

Ce livre existe aussi en français sous le titre :
100 Recettes du temps de Louis XIV
Recettes d'hier au goût d'aujourd'hui

The "Grand Century": a Time of Culinary Innovation

"'I often saw the King (*Louis XIV*) eat four full plates of different soups, a whole pheasant, a partridge, a large plate of salad, two big slices of ham, some mutton cooked with garlic and a full dish pastry, and then still have some fruit and some hard-boiled eggs." [1]
"Dinner was as usual, and Monsieur (*the night before he died*) ate extremely, as he always did at both of his meals, not including the abundant morning chocolate, and all the fruit, pastry, jam and other delicacies, with which his tables, cabinets and pockets were filled all day long."[2]
"We now know that he gave her (*the King's favourite, the Duchess de Berry*) all sorts of things to eat... fricassees, little pasties, salad, milk, figs, plums", all washed down with ice-cold beer." [3] ...

An appetite like that is fascinating. His entourage's bulimia has nothing on Louis XIV's own. A devoted hunter, the King devoured pheasants and partridges. He adored capons, oysters, asparagus, hard-boiled eggs, soups, melons and all manner of sweets. Wherever he was, his table had to be well furnished.

What does that debauchery of food have in common with today's calibrated dishes? Can we really discern in the profusion of that period the roots of today's cooking?
In the 16th century, the Italians had a major influence on European eating habits. Their influence at the time of the Renaissance and of the arrival of Catherine de Medicis (future wife of Henri II) in France, led the French palate to appreciate new flavours. Beans, salads, artichoke hearts, coxcomb and kidneys, sweetmeats, macarons (almond meringues), and marzipan all made their appearance at the royal table at that time.

At the dawn of the 17th century, when agronomist Olivier de Serres was developing new techniques in his domain in Vivarais – growing maize (corn), Piedmont rice and sugar beets – changes were afoot; France was opening to more distant influences, and the concept of cooking was evolving.

Despite certain controversial aspects of his reign, and notwithstanding the opposite extreme, i.e. the French people's poverty and food shortages; it is nevertheless impossible not to acknowledge that Louis XIV played a major role in many different domains, including food.
His century was a pivotal moment in cooking, a moment when the French culinary arts began to find their true personality. Taking advantage of technical evolutions, the preparation of hitherto unknown foodstuffs and unexpected combinations, chefs were bursting with creativity and sharing their new science.

If we take the time to open recipe books from the time – and there were many of them, as we shall see! – we find the seed of many dishes and manners of preparing food that have been perpetuated until our own time.

Chief Steward at the King's Table

Louis XIV was raised in an austere fashion by his mother, Anne of Austria, but upon entering adulthood, he displayed an immense appetite for life and pleasure. Buoyed by common sense and robust physical health, he devoted himself with equally unbridled energy and intensity to work, love, hunting, dancing, and eating and drinking.

His bottomless appetite, an inheritance from the Bourbons that was accentuated by his outdoor lifestyle, led his entourage into an endless quest for novelty. The Court became a laboratory of horticultural and gastronomical research and experimentation that was brought to an acme by its permanent installation at Versailles, in 1682. This newly minted city, which provided jobs to seven or eight thousand people, became the theatre of a never-ending performance. The king wanted to play his own role everywhere at once. Every instant of his life was scheduled and codified: etiquette was all.

Court ceremony was divided into various departments: the Table and the Chamber – the Grand Chamberlain's domain –, the Venery (Hunt), Stables, Ceremonies and Buildings. The entire entourage, a full contingent of domestic positions, was under the direction of the Chief Steward of the King's Household. Maîtres d'Hôtel, Grand Panetier ("Great Bread Master," and the origin of the English word pantry), the Grand Echanson ("Great Cupbearer") carving squires and gentlemen servants: all these offices contributed to the efficient functioning of the King's Table department of the Royal Household.

The royal day was punctuated by meals: in the morning, for breakfast, Louis XIV has a bit of wine, water and bread. At noon, dinner was served to a small or very small number of people in the King's Chamber; if there were more guests, it would be in the first antechamber. Dinner, when it was for a large number of people, and supper, at 10 p.m., became a sort of performance, but one presented on a set where the audience was standing and the actor seated. The ceremony was precisely regulated: the king ate facing the "audience", men wore hats and carried swords. The organisation of the "spectacle", established even before the King's installation at Versailles, was unchanging: "The gentleman servant carries the first dish; the second is carried by the Controller; the Officers of the King's Table take the others. In this order, the Maître d'Hôtel, with baton in hand and carrying a baguette, and in the evening carrying a torch as well, opens the march, preceding the Usher by a few steps to the table; the meat, surrounded by three bodyguards, rifles at the ready, having arrived, the Maître d'Hôtel bows to the Nave. 4". The trajectory that the Meat follows from the kitchens to the King's table, is so long that the meat must be kept covered. The King's Cupbearer pours the wine and the water.

When there were "soirées d'appartement" – occasions for entertainment inaugurated at Versailles – buffets of beverages were arranged in the Salon de l'Abondance and collations in the Venus antechamber. Elisabeth-Charlotte de Bavière, the Princess Palatine, Louis XIV's sister-in-law, to whom we owe a caustic chronicle of Court life, said she found them deadly.

For this endless performance, above and beyond abundance and profusion, the dishes had to be chosen with care, prepared according to strict rules and arranged according to precise criteria. Mediocrity was not acceptable. The quest for balance and harmony that can be seen in the construction of Versailles was also applied to the table. Everything had to be perfect.

The table, like a jardin à la française, had to compose a harmonious, symmetrical picture, taking into account form, colour and the nature of each food. The dishes, geometrically arranged, created an oval, circular, triangular, square or rectangular pattern. Officers had recourse to "flying plates", raised dishes allowing them to present fruit and sweetmeats in pyramid shapes. Flowers, citrus fruit and salads added touches of colour à la decoration. La Quintinie, for whom the fruit's intrinsic qualities were all that really mattered, ironically described those pyramids of fruit in which appearance was everything, "and which are no less useful for that, if only to do honour to the Officer who arranged them with such symmetry." 5

During fêtes, among the incessantly unfolding displays of waterworks, illuminations, fireworks, ballets and concerts, between the groves and fountains, the shape and layout of the tables was of the utmost importance. At the Grande Fête "Pleasures of the Enchanted Island," held at Versailles in May, 1664, six hundred courtesans applauded Molière plays and Lulli ballets and nibbled delicacies presented on a tables shaped like crescent moons to match the Ariosto's "Orlando furioso" theme that ran through the entire celebration.

Faux pas were simply not acceptable: the art of the maître d'hôtel and the gardener, like those of the musician or the architect, were considered hard sciences. Harmony was the rule, balance the norm, and symmetry proof of success.

To achieve this degree of perfection, Louis XIV had to surround himself with key people who were able to build for him and for France a sort of ideal world in which every person, every thing and every moment had its place and was in it. This regulation of the slightest detail was not due to Colbert alone. "Academianism", of which he was undoubtedly one of the pillars, was applied in every domain.

The king, an eagle-eyed observer of human nature, constantly on the lookout for anyone able to live up to his expectations and serve his ambitions, made some top-notch catches. He could pride himself on having brought in to build and run Versailles Le Nôtre, Hardouin-Mansart, Le Brun, Molière, Lulli, Le Vau, Racine, Boileau, La Fontaine, and many more…

… Including Jean-Baptiste de La Quintinie. "I have lost a friend", Louis XIV said to Quintinie's wife at the death of the man he called "Monsieur le Jardinier". Born in Charente in 1626, lawyer at the Parliament of Paris, La Quintinie didn't discover his horticultural vocation until accepting a position as preceptor for the son of Jean Tambonneau, president of the Chamber of Accounts. Tambonneau lived in a stately home on Faubourg Saint-Germain, built to plans drawn by Le Vau. It was set in the midst of vast gardens laid out by Le Nôtre, where the jurist first undertook his observations and experimentation. He completed them through his travels, particularly in Italy, and would work on embellishing a great number of properties and châteaux, most notably for the Prince of Condé. For "Monsignor Colbert's" property at Sceaux (south of Paris) he laid out "one of the most beautiful vegetable gardens that has ever been seen": by his own account, "This kitchen garden is so perfect that there is nothing mediocre about it, nor anything that should be disavowed, as it is true that nowhere can be found healthier, more vigorous trees; more excellent or beautiful fruit, nor tastier vegetables."

Catching the attention of Louis XIV, who lingered in the kitchen garden at Sceaux on a visit to his minister, La Quintinie was called by the king to care for the kitchen garden that Louis XIII had had planted at Versailles. In May, 1670, he received the title of steward of the royal orchards and vegetable gardens and was named Officer of the King's House. Ten years later, he designed the King's Vegetable Garden on 20 acres (8 hectares) of land allocated in place of a drained pond near the Swiss Guard's lake. It was on this land, living in a house designed for him by Mansart, that he carefully, meticulously and lovingly grew and ripened the fruit, salads, vegetables and herbs that honoured the table of Louis XIV. The former lawyer divided the land into a series of walled gardens. The walls, covered with espaliered fruit trees, protected the plants from the wind. In this way, he created thirty-one distinct gardens, each one dedicated to one or more specialities: asparagus, strawberries, melons, figs, cucumbers and lettuce. The central garden covered 7.5 acres (3 hectares).

"This large square, drawn by the Cartesian mind of the century, was divided into sixteen smaller squares, three of which were planted with summer pears, three in autumn pears, and the ten others in winter pears. Raised terraces surrounded this orchard. Their walls were all covered in grapevines." 6

A lover of trees, the king learned the golden rules of pruning from his gardener. A taste for good fruit had been inherited along with the crown: Anne of Austria passed this love on to her son, and received from Mr. Arnaud d'Andilly, an old friend of La Quintinie's, baskets laden with fruits from the king's orchard at Port Royal des Champs.

La Quintinie also managed to acclimatise orange trees, another one of the king's passions, which he had brought in from distant lands, but which he never managed to bring to fruition.

"Orange trees, trees I adore,

Your flowers perfume the air I breathe," wrote La Fontaine at the time.

For himself, for his gardeners, and in homage to his teacher, La Quintinie set the rules of his art down in his *Instructions for Fruit and Vegetable Gardens*, published posthumously.

A tree should be balanced, good fruit must of necessity be beautiful fruit. Mastery of every detail, from the soil to the harvest, is essential.

Reading his *Instructions* is revealing: one comes across the words good, perfect, delicious, excellent, etc. ... on every line. "Among the fruits currently available in the world's commerce," the author wrote, "we can say unequivocally that there are such exquisite and perfect ones that nothing more delicious to the taste buds could be known, and perhaps nothing better for the health, either."

With expectations so high, the "disaster" caused by the late arrival of fresh seafood was, for Vatel, Nicolas Fouquet's maître d'hôtel – and mastermind behind the banquet given by Condé for the king on 17 August, 1671 – a setback so dramatic that only his spectacular suicide could redeem it, in a gesture symbolic of this desperate search for perfection.

Thus, as is ever the case, under the rule of a centralising sovereign, who encouraged artistic talents to serve his own power and to make his realm one which would be held up as an example to posterity, the Court's cooking also started certain trends – at least in high society. In 1691, François Massialot entitled his cookbook *The Royal and Bourgeois Chef*, and introduced high-ranking persons' names into the titles of his recipes. Just as Louis XIV enjoyed pruning trees, some of his lords and courtesans liked to cook. Mme de Sable, for example, whose excellent table was held in high repute: Philippe d'Orleans was said to have enjoyed dining there; his son, the future Regent, also cooked: fish stews and omelettes. Even the King's Secretary, Louis de Bechameil, who invented Bechamel sauce.

Let us not forget the superintendent and director of the Academy of Music, Jean-Baptiste Lulli. He began his career as a kitchen boy for the Grande Mademoiselle. Or Mr. de L'Estang, "candle snuffer" in Molière's troupe, born Cyprien Ragueneau in 1608 and later immortalised by Edmond Rostand in *Cyrano de Bergerac*, was an occasional poet and actor, but above all a pastry chef who attracted – thanks to his verses or his almond tarts? – literary bohemia. In classical times, it seems, theatre, cooking and music went very well together.

To this day, we are still enjoying the heritage from this era. Let's learn how to savour it from the masters of the "Grand Century".

New Flavours, New Foods

After the era of exploration and discovery of the late 15th and 16th centuries, relations with distant lands were beginning to be established on a commercial basis.

In 1664, Colbert, who believed that colonies should provide raw materials as well as becoming markets for French products, successively founded the French West India Company and, hoping to outstrip the Portuguese, Dutch and English who had already been established there for quite some time, the French East India Company. Through them and other colonial enterprises, hitherto unknown or extremely rare products, generally from the tropics, gradually became more widespread: importation of spices, pepper, cinnamon and anise, was simplified. Cane sugar, which the French produced in great quantities in the Antilles, through the practice of "peopling" (immigration) and slavery (regulated by a series of laws known as "the black code"), was taxed from September, 1664.

Countries were opening up. Visits from ambassadors of distant lands, like those of Siam, who, in 1686, tasted La Quintinie's muscat grapes, "which they found lovely", as well as the tales of travellers – like François Bernier, Jean-Baptiste Tavernier, upon whom Louis XIV conferred a title of nobility, and Jean Chardin – revealed extraordinary customs. In their footsteps came the surprise of new flavours and, in their endless seeking for originality and exoticism, the rich made new, unknown flavours, foods and beverages fashionable.

The king's infatuation with novel and unexpected tastes was yet another key to this evolution.

Chocolate, which Cortez had tasted in Mexico, arrived in the trunks of the Infanta Maria-Theresa, daughter of Philip IV of Spain, when she was wed to Louis XIV in 1660. It would, for some time, be consumed as a hot or cold beverage, one which both the queen, and her rival, Mme de Maintenon, adored. Its medicinal qualities made it ideal for "modifying vapours from the spleen". Upon leaving the apothecary domain, its method of consumption would gradually evolve: Philippe Du Four, specialist in the international commerce of "drugs" from the Orient, noted that it was taken "as a solid" and that the Italians drank it "with ice" [7]. In 1691, Massialot became the first person on record to use it as an ingredient in cooking.

Coffee – known to those who had travelled in Arabia, sipped in Constantinople and appreciated by the Venetians from the early 17th century – arrived in Marseilles in 1643, before being introduced to the Court by the Ambassador of Turkey, and then to Paris where, in 1686, the Sicilian Procopio de Cotellin opened his café, Procope, which is still flourishing today. Yet coffee was not universally appreciated; on 22 July, 1714, the Princess Palatine exclaimed indignantly: "It never ceases to amaze me how many people like coffee; yet its taste is horribly unpleasant." [8]. Tea, which came from Macao and was less widespread at the time, was imported via Portugal or the Netherlands, and was prescribed by Fagon, the King's Doctor, for his patient.

Even the vineyards of Ile-de-France (the Paris region), which, in 1600, covered more than 50,000 acres, had to ward off competition from wines arriving from foreign countries. On princely tables, syrupy grands crus from Spain – Malvoisie, Malaga, Alicante and Xerès – were served alongside the highly reputed wines of Burgundy – Beaune, Irancy, Vertus – Bordeaux and Champagne… which was not yet a sparkling wine. They came from Brittany or via the sea. Hungarian Tokay was all the rage at Versailles.

Louis XIV's unflagging curiosity – "Louis XIV, all his life, enquired. He had to have the answer to all the questions he asked" [9] – as well as his attraction for all things new and novel, encouraged the development in France of vegetables like asparagus, cauliflower from Cypres, green peas, which Audiger brought back from Italy in 1660, and fruit, whose varieties multiplied, like melons, figs, and peaches. Colbert's letters reflect the concerns of La Quintinie, constantly seeking novelties for the king and his vegetable garden. In a letter dated November 1670, the Minister solicited M. Arnoud, intendant of the Marseilles Shipyards: "I impatiently await the tuberoses, muscat grapes and currants that you have promised me. Search carefully for all flowers and plants, both known and unknown; if you come across them in foreign lands, be sure to do so, and to make arrangements early enough to be able to send them to me in large quantities next year."[10]

Experiments were appreciated, discoveries were adored. And the king loved to share his enthusiasms and infatuations: "His Majesty having been gracious enough to share his satisfaction (with the peas) commanded me to bring them to Lord Baudoin, controller of the King's Table, and to tell him to prepare a small dish of them for the Queen Mother, one for the Queen, one for Monsignor the Cardinal and the rest should be kept for Monsieur to eat with Her", Audiger explained. In his Relating of the Fête at Versailles on eighteen July sixteen-hundred and sixty-eight, celebrating the peace of Aix-la-Chapelle, at a time when citrus fruit was still a rare and precious commodity, André Félibien marvelled to see "a magnificent collation of oranges from Portugal and all sorts of fruits, piled high in thirty-six baskets and in pyramids".

This wide variety of flavours went hand in hand with a growing attention to maintaining the specific qualities of the ingredients used to prepare dishes. The refinement of the gardeners, of whom La Quintinie was one of the teachers, seeking in the King's vegetable garden the ideal ripeness of each fruit or vegetable, incited the cooks to find ways of preparing them which preserved and highlighted the produce's natural flavour, rather than masking the taste with too many different flavours.

How could Louis XIV not have developed his gustatory sensuality, with a guide capable of explaining in his instructions to gardeners: "The first virtue of peaches is to have flesh just barely firm (...) flesh which must be fine, shiny and bright yellow, without the slightest trace of green (...) The next virtue of peaches is that this flesh should melt as soon as it is in the mouth, for peach flesh is in fact no more than frozen water which reverts to a liquid state as soon as it is pressed between the teeth ..." [12]

As early as 1654, Nicolas de Bonnefons, horticulturist and yet another specialist in vegetable gardens, advised housewives to maintain the "natural taste", the "true taste": "Try whenever possible to diversify and distinguish by taste and shape what you prepare; let a health soup be a good bourgeois soup, nourished with good, well-chosen meats and reduced to little bouillon, with no chopped meat, mushrooms, spices, or other ingredients, but keep it simple, since it is bears the name of health; let cabbage soup taste entirely of cabbage; leek, of leek; turnip, of turnip; and so on and so forth with all others".[13]

Sweet-savoury blends, frequent in earlier centuries, began to be looked down upon, and the use of spices became subtler. L.S.R., the mysterious author of L' *Art de bien traiter* ("The Art of Preparing Well", see below), waxed ironic about the lingering taste for sweet sauces: "If someone likes and request a sweet sauce – which to me is the height of impertinence, and ridiculous to boot – you can satisfy him by boiling some red wine with sugar, cloves and cinnamon, and reduce everything to the consistency of syrup." [14]

Butter began to attract notice and to be used instead of beef marrow in certain regions and at well-to-do tables.

Of course, all this would hardly have been found in peasants' porringers. Not counting times of food shortages and famines (let us not forget that out of a population of twenty million, some one million six hundred thousand people died of hunger, disease and epidemics in France in 1693-1694!), one would find: soups, sometimes enriched with a bit of bacon; fish, whether saltwater for those who lived by the sea, or fresh; hares, generally poached; flat cakes made with all different flours; porridges, crêpes, chick peas, root vegetables, garlic and onion. But we can also get a whiff of the well-to-do peasants' feasts described by Pierre Goubert: "Now the soup had the rich smell of bacon, or even ham, plus butter, oil or lard; here it was made with cabbage, there with peas, yet elsewhere with tomatoes or other sun-drenched vegetables. Dried sausage or smoked pork as well, grouse or capon, the plump Christmas bird, the Pascal lamb, sometimes a poule au pot on Sunday (...) And to finish these feasts, or rich *man's meals*, diverse crêpes, fritters, merveilles, pets de nonnes, pies, puddings, gingerbreads and brioches ..."[15]

From Pan to Pen

In this era of monarchic art, in which an official style became codified, every aspect of social life – at Court essentially – followed rules. The culinary arts had, in their way, to bow to etiquette too. Good taste and good food were like literature: not only was the order and service of meals pre-established, as we have seen, but so were the contents of each dish, and the work in the 'offices' or different roles in the kitchen. Thus did rules become formalised for how to prepare the best sauce or cook soup to perfection. And these recipes were written down, allowing the authors to guide novice cooks and to address an ever-increasing bourgeois audience.

French cuisine gradually found its own unique style, freeing itself from the Italian influence that had been predominant in the previous century.

Except for a few treatises, most often intended for carving squires, it wasn't until the middle of the 17th century that books dispensing recipes and tips for cooks at rich or bourgeois tables began to appear. Let us mention those which gained the most notoriety and which were our principal sources in choosing the recipes that follow.

The Marquis d'Uxelles' kitchen squire, François Pierre, better known by his nickname, La Varenne, paved the way in 1651. Le *Cuisinier françois, enseignant la maniere de bien apprester & assaisonner toutes sortes de viandes grasses & maigres, legumes, patisseries, & autres mets qui se servent tant sur les tables des grands que des particuliers,* ("The French Chef, teaching the art and the manner of preparing and seasoning all sorts of fat and lean meats, vegetables, pastry, & other foodstuffs served at both grand tables an in private homes"), published be Pierre David, contained some 700 recipes: soups, starters, roasts, side dishes, bouillons, juices and jams. La Varenne grants vegetables a place of honour, and his recipes aim to highlight the ingredients' natural taste. With its clear organisation and well-structured chapters, the book was a huge success, and it was reprinted in 1652. Nearly thirty reprints would follow! We could say that La Varenne inaugurated the nouvelle cuisine of his century.

That same year, a valet in the King's Chamber, but above all a horticulturist, Nicolas de Bonnefons, wrote a treatise dedicated essentially preserving fruit in light syrup, but which also contained recipes for candied and crystallised fruit: Le *Jar.   ançois, qui enseigne à cultiver les arbres, & herbes potageres ; avec la maniere de*

conserver les fruicts, & faire toutes sortes de confitures, conserves, & massepans. Dedie aux dames. ("The French Gardener, which teaches to cultivate fruit trees and edible herbs; including the art and manner of preserving fruits and all sorts of jams, preserves and marzipans. For ladies.")
In 1654 he would follow it up with another recipe book: *Les Delices de la campagne*, ("Delights of the Countryside") in which, though he was not a cook, he explained how to make bread ("the most vital of all the Foodstuffs"); pastry; wines and beverages; and even *botriphagy*, (*"the eating of Roots"*); fruit and vegetables; eggs and dairy products, and finally meat, poultry and fish.

The author of Le *Pastissier françois ; où est enseigne la maniere de faire toute sorte de pastisserie, tres-utile à toutes personnes* ("The French Pastry Chef; in which is taught the art and the manner of making all sorts of pastry – very useful for all persons") (published in 1653 by Jean Gaillard) has never been identified with certitude. Without mentioning professionals, it is addressed to bourgeois who enjoy making pastry. Unlike this others, this volume, the first one dedicated exclusively to pastry (both sweet and savoury, with recipes for flaky pastry, puff pastry and more...), more often than not includes practical details like cooking time, units of measure and proportions.

1656: Pierre de Lune Le *Nouveau Cuisinier, où il est traite de la veritable methode pour apprester toutes sortes de viandes, gibbier, volatiles, poissons, tant de mer que d'eau douce : suivant les quatres saisons de l'annee. Ensemble la maniere de faire toutes sortes de patisseries, tant froides que chaudes, en perfection* ("The New Cook, in which is explained the true method for preparing all sorts of meats, game, poultry, fish – both fresh- and saltwater – following the four seasons of the year. Including also the manner for making all sorts of pastries, both cold and warm, to perfection", publisher: Pierre David).

The author, to whom the president of the Court of Aides, Jacques Amelot de Mauregard, wrote, "I can say that I found therein the secret to pleasing the most difficult palate," [17] almost undoubtedly practised his art first for the Duke of Rohan, then for the Duchess if Orleans, before going independent. Among his 900 recipes, a considerable number, he propose a profusion of sweet and savoury pies, and true to 16th-century tastes, includes an abundance of coxcombs and artichoke hearts, of which Catherine de Medicis was known to have been inordinately fond.
L'Escole Parfaite des officiers de bouche ; contenant le vray maistre-d'hostel, le grand escuyer-tranchant, le sommelier royal, le confiturier royal, le cuisinier royal, et le pastissier royal, ("The Perfect School of Officers of the King's Table; including the true maître d'hotel, the grand carving squire, the royal sommelier, the royal jam-maker, the royal chef, and the royal pastry chef"), published in 1662 by Veuve Pierre David & Ribou, would seem to be an anthology of several treatises about the different offices of the King's Table. Its global nature earned it tremendous success until 1742.

In 1674, *L'Art de bien traiter. Divise en trois parties. Ouvrage nouveau, curieux, et fort galant, utile à toutes personnes, et conditions.* ("The Art of Preparing Well: Divided into three parts. A New, Open-Minded and Gallant Work, useful for all persons and conditions") The author: L.S.R. Initials of Sir Rolland, officer of the Table of Princess de Carignan, or of Sir Robert?
As a caustic critic of La Varenne, who he found too fussy, L.S.R. simplifies preparations, without losing their refinement. His recipes often end with suggestions for presentation, as food should please the eyes as well as the palate. He also was against excessive sweet-and-savoury combinations and overdoing spices; L.S.R. advises the use of butter and, like his predecessors, encourages cooking styles that preserve foods' true taste.

Late in the century, in 1691, François Massialot, a little-known figure, took over from La Varenne with *Le Cuisinier roïal et bourgeois, Qui apprend à ordonner toute sorte de Repas, & la meilleur maniere des Ragoûts les plus à la mode & les plus exquis. Ouvrage tres-utile dans les Familles, & singulierement necessaire à tous Maîtres d'Hôtels, & Ecuïers de Cuisine.* ("Royal and Bourgeois Cuisine, which teaches how to serve all sorts of Meals, the most fashionable Ragouts and the most exquisite dishes. A very useful work for Families, and a singularly necessary one for Maiîres d'Hôtels and Kitchen Squires") Included with this exhaustive collection of recipes, the author also proposes many menus for full meals. There is great variety in his cuisine, which highlights all the ingredients recently introduced at the Court of Versailles.

The following year, Massialot wrote yet another cookbook: Nouvelle instruction pour les confitures, les liqueurs et les fruits. Egalement utile dans les familles, pour savoir ce qu'on sert de plus à la mode dans les repas, & en d'autres occasions ("New instruction for jams, liqueurs and fruits. Equally useful for families, for knowing what is served at fashionable meals & other occasions").

Audiger, the one who introduced Louis XIV to peas, served the aristocracy before opening a café in Paris. In 1692, thanks to his experience as an officer in a noble household, he freely dispensed advice and recipes in La Maison reglee, et l'art de diriger la maison d'un grand Seigneur & autres, tant à la Ville qu'à la Campagne, & le devoir de tous les Officiers, & autres Domestiques en general. Avec la veritable methode de faire toutes sortes d'Essences, d'Eaux et de Liqueurs, fortes & rafraîchissantes, à la mode d'Italie. Ouvrage utile et necessaire à toutes sortes de personnes de qualite, Gentilshommes de Provinces, Etrangers, Bourgeois, Officiers de grandes Maisons, Limonadiers & autres Marchands de Liqueurs ("The Well-Run Household, the Art of Running a Great Lord's House or others, in the City or the Country, & the Role of all the Officers, & other Domestics in general. With the veritable method for making all sorts of strong & refreshing Essences, Eaux & Liqueurs, in the Italian style. A useful and necessary book for all people of quality, Gentlemen of the Provinces, Foreigners, Bourgeois, Officers of Great Houses, Café Owners & other Liqueur Merchant").

Other books containing recipes appeared around this time: 'office' books, jam books (including digestive beverages, pickled foods, jams and sweetmeats, as well as pommades, soaps and fragrances), books about new beverages. Editorial production continued to develop considerably, highlighting to what extent readers', at least specialised ones, sensibilities had been opened to this innovative approach to the culinary arts, traces of which can still be found in our plates today.

Innovation at the Stove: ragouts, bisques, sherbets and pressure cookers

It wasn't until the early 17th century that architects began to propose integrating the needs of the table into the layout of aristocratic homes in a rational manner: kitchen, 'office' (a cooler, dryer room), larder. In addition, for the very rich, there could be: "bake-house, bread oven, wine cellar, fruit cellar, laundry room and drapery closet". The dining room as one reserved exclusively for meals didn't appear until around 1630 [18].

In L'Architecture françoise de bastimens particuliers ("French Architecture for private buildings"), published in 1624, Louis Savot devoted a long chapter to the building of an ice-cellar, for "preserving ice, to use during the warmest parts of summer", a technique that was becoming widespread in France, and which allowed not only for keeping beverages cool, but for the trend for sherbet recipes. Audiger also suggests one his La Maison reglee ("The Well-Run Household"), in 1692.

Cooking methods were also starting to change.

Roasting had become more modern in the previous century thanks to leather bellows and spring-and-weight roasting spits. In the "grand century", the question of preserving food's taste was on everyone's mind, to the extent that even physicians considered the issue.

Thus, in the year 1682, a physician whose name is still known, in the footsteps of the Englishman Boyle who invented a screw-tight double boiler, looked into how best to cook food. Denis Papin came up with a "digester", a hermetically sealed recipient containing water, which, when brought to the boil, released steam that would cook meat or vegetables. "Through the means of this machine, the oldest, toughest cow can be made as tender and tasty as the best-chosen meat" [19], according to the inventor, who was particularly attached to the idea that, no matter what he tries to cook with it – meat, fish, vegetables or fruit – the cooked food's taste keeps more of its strength. The pressure cooker had not yet been invented and cooks didn't yet have recourse to this modern cooking technique, but Denis Papin tried to present it to the King for his Armies and for the poor.

Another technique that would renew the art of pastry making and open up numerous new paths: an innovation in Le Pâtissier françois, which, in 1653, suggested the use of air to thicken egg whites in recipes like œufs à la neige and whipped cream.

The organisation of meals also evolved during the 17th century.

Along with the gradual disappearance of sweet meat, fish and vegetables, we can notice that the serving order iwa modified and simplified. During meals, practically all fruit is now served for dessert. And, according to Pierre de Lune, the number of courses dropped to five: *potage*, entrée, Roast, side dish and dessert.

In this context conducive to innovation, all the ingredients needed for change came together: new tastes, focus on authentic flavours, evolution of techniques, importance bestowed on meals. A few classic dishes appeared, thanks to the skills of La Varenne, Pierre de Lune or François Massialot. The 17th *century's nouvelle cuisine* would become our cuisine. You'll find myriad examples in the pages that follow. Let us mention but a few: bisque, fish au bleu, *bœuf mode*, *roux*, sunny-side up eggs and the "packet" – now known as a *bouquet garni*.
Cook-poets, like Cesar Pellenc, head chef for the governor of Apt, Hector de Brancas (and perhaps his *nom de plume* as well), knew how to sing the praises of these novel dishes, like bisque:
"*Grand mets des plus honnestes gens* (...), / Grand dish for honest men,
Potage qui vaut tant d'escus, / Soup worth many a coin,
Bouillon des gosiers à couronne, / Bouillon fit for the throat of the king,
Pour toy je quitterois quatre mille autre jus./ For you I would leave 4,000 other drinks" [20]
This is how we see this founding period in our culinary tradition. We have inherited myriad cookbooks, source of numerous recipes for today.

The Grand Siècle, notes

1 Quoted by D. Meyer, *Quand les rois régnaient à Versailles*. ("When kings reigned in Versailles")
2 Saint-Simon, *Mémoires*, 1701; "Monsieur" was Louis XIV's only brother.
3 1719 - *Letters from the Princess Palatine, 1672-1722.*
4 The Nave was a tray containing the King's plate, spoon and knife; Louis XIV didn't use forks, and forbade those close to him to do so either. In D. Meyer, *Quand les rois régnaient à Versailles*, p. 47.
5 *Instructions pour les jardins*, t. I, trois. partie. About La Quintinie, see below.
6 J. Gervais, *Le Jardinier du Roi*, p. 78.
7 *Traitez nouveaux & curieux du café, du thé et du chocolat*, 1685, see *Livres en bouche*, p. 152.
8 Letters from the Princess Palatine, 1672-1722.
9 J. Gervais, *Le Jardinier du Roi*.
10 Dans J. Gervais, *op. cit.*
11 Quoted by J. Ferniot, *L'Europe à table*.
12 La Quintinie, *Instructions pour les jardins*, t. I, trois. partie, ch. X.
13 *Les Délices de la campagne*, quoted in *Livres en bouche*, p. 125 (see below).
14 Quoted in Livres en bouche, p. 109.
15 *La vie quotidienne des paysans français au XVIIe siècle.* ("Daily Life of 17th Century French Peaasants")
16 For this part, we owe a great deal to the remarkable catalogue of the exhibit *Livres en bouche* ("Tasty Books") that was held at the Bibliothèque de l'Arsenal in Paris in 2001-2002 (see bibliogr.).
17 Quoted in *Livres en bouche*, p. 139.
18 Voir Livres en bouche, pp. 132-133.
19 Ibid.
20 In *Les Plaisirs de la vie*, ("Life's Pleasures")1655, quoted in *Livres en bouche*.

 Menu

*Table with two dishes and two settings, for the first season
(January, February, March)*

*Pierre de Lune, Le nouveau et parfait Maistre d'hostel royal,
("The New and Perfect Royal Maitre d'Hotel") 1662*

Un potage de santé, & une bisque que vous poserez/A health soup, & a bisque

Un potage de santé/A health soup

Un potage de ramiers aux chous/A cabbage soup

Un potage de sarcelles/A Sarcelles soup

Entrées/Starters

Un poulet d'Inde lardé de gros lard en ragoust/Ragout of turkey with bacon

Un ragoust de canards/Duck ragout

Ragoust de petits pigeonneaux/Ragout of young pigeons

De testes d'agneaux frits/Fried Head of Lamb

Rosty/Roasts

Chapons & faisans/Capons & Pheasants

Poulets & perdrix/Chickens & Partridges

Cailles bardées & pigeons piquez/Larded Quail & Pigeon

Pluviers & mauviettes/Skylark & Plover

Trois salades diferentes sur la saliere/Three different salads

Entre-mets à quatre assiettes pour plat/Four Seasons of Side Dishes

Une de ris de veau - Une de champignons/One of veal - One of mushrooms

Une assiette de montans - Une de baignets/One of fritters

Une assiette de cresme à la Reyne - Une de gelée de grenade
A dish of Queen's Custard/One of Pomegranate Jelly

Une de crestes - Une de truffes en ragoust/One of coxcombs - One of truffle ragout

Une assiette de pieds de porc- Une de langues de porc
A plate of pigs' trotters - One of pigs' tongues

Starters & Hors d'œuvres

*F*ried-Egg Civet (Stew)

Prenez des œufs et les faites frire tout entiers, et sans les rompre, dans de la bonne huile. Ayez aussi des oignons, tranchez-les par rouelles et les faites frire de même que les œufs; mettez-y du verjus, du vin et du vinaigre, et faites bouillir le tout ensemble. Cela fait, ayez plusieurs écuelles et dans chacune mettez 3 ou 4 de vos œufs et votre brouet par-dessus et faites en sorte qu'il soit clairet.

L'Escole parfaite des Officiers de bouche, 1662

SERVES 6

6 eggs

3 fresh onions

1 clove garlic, peeled and crushed

25 cl./1 cup red wine

5 cl. + 2 Tbsp./ ⅕ cup + 2 Tbsp. oil

a drizzle of vinegar

1 Tbsp. flour

a few sprigs of parsley

sat & pepper to taste

Peel and mince the onions. Fry them for about 5 minutes in a pan with the 2 tablespoons of oil. Add the peeled and crushed garlic. Sprinkle the onions and garlic with flour, moisten everything with a bit of vinegar, then pour the wine in, stirring carefully to avoid lumps. Salt and pepper to taste, add the parsley, which should be removed before serving. Stir for a moment, then let it simmer gently for 15 to 20 minutes, checking occasionally that it's not burning or sticking.

While this brouet ("thin soup", here the wine sauce) is cooking, fry the eggs one by one, "whole, and without breaking them." Start by breaking them into a ramekin. Heat the remaining 5 cl / ⅕ cup of oil in a small frying pan. As soon as the oil starts to smoke, tip the pan and slip the egg gently into the oil. Keep the white close to the yolk and turn the egg over easy with a spatula or a small skimmer. Once it's cooked, keep it warm while you prepare the next ones.

Place each egg in a serving dish and garnish with the onion sauce. You can serve this starter with lightly toasted slices of farmhouse bread.

Cucumber Salad

La Varenne, Le cuisinier françois, 1651

SERVES 6

1 cucumber
1 shallot
2 Tbsp. olive oil
1 Tbsp. vinegar
1 small bunch chives
5 sprigs chervil
salt & white pepper to taste

Peel the cucumber and slice it very thin. Place the slices in a large bowl.

Season with the salt, white pepper and vinegar and add the finely chopped shallot. Leave the preparation in a cool place for at least an hour.

Just before serving, drizzle generously with olive oil and sprinkle with freshly chopped herbs.

Stuffed Cucumber Soup

Pierre de Lune, Le Cuisinier, 1656

Fish Mussels

La Varenne, Le cuisinier françois, 1651

SERVES 6

1 kg 500/3 lbs. bouchot mussels (cultivated on pilings at sea)
50 g/ ¼ cup fresh butter
1 large shallot
1 bouquet garni (thyme, parsley and bay leaf)
a few sprigs flat-leaf parsley
1 small bunch fresh chives
a few sprigs chervil
1 pinch of grated nutmeg
3 egg yolks
juice of ½ lemon

Clean the mussels carefully then place them in a large pot with the bouquet garni. Cover and cook at high heat, shaking the pot from time to time.

As soon as the mussels open, turn off the heat and let them cool. Shell them, setting aside the six nicest shells for garnishing the dish. Strain the lemon juice and set aside.

Peel and mince the shallot, cook them gently in the butter until they turn a nice golden brown. Add the drained mussels, the nutmeg and the chopped parsley and chives. Stir everything together well for one minute, then remove the pan from the heat.

In a small pot, whip the egg yolks with a few spoonfuls of the mussel juice. Simmer gently for a few minutes, then add the lemon juice. If the sauce is too thick, thin it with some more mussel juice. Adjust the seasoning. Warm a serving dish before arranging the mussels in the centre, and decorating with the reserved shells around the rim. Pour the sauce over everything and sprinkle with a bit of chervil. Serve immediately.

$\mathcal{A}$sparagus Omelette

One of Louis XIV's favourite dishes, asparagus received a tremendous amount of tender loving care from La Quintinie, who perfected a way of keeping them warm by growing them under glass, "to add to this little chef-d'oeuvre's dramatic effect." "In all modesty I can say," he wrote, "that I was the first, thanks to some plausible reasoning, to have attempted this innovation, in order to bring the greatest King in the world a hitherto unknown pleasure."(Instructions for Gardens, t. II, part six, ch. III).
Pierre de Lune accommodates them with eggs in a simple but delicious recipe.

SERVES 6

500 g/1 lb. green asparagus
1 small onion, chopped
12 eggs
20 cl/1 cup heavy cream
50 g/3 Tbsp. cup butter
1 bouquet fresh chives
2 sprigs thyme
a few sprigs flat-leaf parsley, chopped
1 pinch grated nutmeg
salt & pepper to taste

Clean the asparagus and cut them into 2-cm./1-inch long pieces. In a large pan, sauté them quickly in 25 g/1½ Tbsp. of butter. Add the chopped onion and half the chopped parsley and chives, as well as the nutmeg and the thyme needles.

Season to taste with the salt and pepper, and cook on medium heat for 15 minutes, stirring frequently. While the asparagus are cooking, beat the eggs with the heavy cream and the rest of the herbs. Season to taste; add the cooked asparagus to the eggs.

Melt 25 g/1½ Tbsp. of butter in the same pan and pour in the eggs and asparagus. Let it cook on very low heat until the omelette is moist but not runny, about 20 minutes. Serve hot or cold, with a green salad, and seasoned with lemon-and-orange-juice vinaigrette.

Our Tip
Choose extra-thin green asparagus that don't require peeling. Just cut off the gritty end before use.

*P*ortuguese Style Pâté

Pierre de Lune, Le Cuisinier, 1636

SERVES 6

2 rolls of ready-made puff/flaky (croissant-type) pastry

250 g/ ½ lb. turkey breast

200 g / 4/10 lb. cultivated mushrooms

1 shallot

5 prunes

5 dates

2 Tbsp. currants/small black raisins

50 g/ 1.75 oz. / ½ cup shelled pistachio nuts

1 lemon peel

1 pinch cinnamon

3 Tbsp. olive oil

20 g./1 Tbsp. butter

1 egg yolk

salt & pepper to taste

FOR THE (OPTIONAL) GLAZE

2 Tbsp. orange-blossom water

1 Tbsp. sugar

Pre-heat your oven to 175°C/350° F./Gas Mark ¾ Chop the turkey breast, the cleaned mushrooms, the peeled shallot and the lemon peel. Add the roughly chopped prunes and dates, the whole pistachios and the currants/raisins. Mix well, pour in the olive oil and season with the salt and pepper.

Cut an approximately equal-sized dolphin shape out of each of the rolls of pastry dough. Lay the larger one on your buttered baking sheet. Spread the turkey mixture onto it, being careful not to get too close to the edges. Cover the filling with the second pastry, and seal the edges carefully. Brush the surface with the egg yolk thinned with a tablespoon of water. Lightly cut a criss-cross pattern into the top crust with the tip of a sharp knife. Cut a small "chimney" into the centre to let steam escape. Bake for 1¼ hours. When the crust starts to brown, cover it lightly with a sheet of aluminium foil.

If you wish, brush it with Pierre de Lune's proposed sugar-and-orange-blossom water glaze.

$\mathcal{F}$ried Marinated Chicken

Coupez petits poulets par petits morceaux, décharnez les os tant que vous pourrez pourvu qu'ils tiennent à la chair, les mettez tremper dans vinaigre, sel, poivre, un paquet, citron vert, et laurier, faites une pate avec farine, eau, et sel, trempez les morceaux de poulets dedans, puis les faire frire en lart fondu, puis servez à la persillade et tranches de citron.

Pierre de Lune, Le Cuisinier, 1656

Here is the ancestor of the fried chicken that is so popular with children worldwide nowadays.

SERVES 6

2 young hens
oil for frying
salt, pepper
2 lemons

FOR THE MARINADE

Juice of 3 limes
3 cloves garlic
1 shallot
3 sprigs thyme
1 bunch flat-leaf parsley
1 bay leaf
2 Tbsp. wine vinegar
10 cl/ 1/3 cup dry white wine
3 Tbsp. olive oil

FOR THE BREADING

150 g/ 1 1/3 cup flour
1 tsp. salt
1 tsp. ground pepper
1 pinch powdered ginger
1 pinch paprika
1 tsp. dried oregano

Set aside a few stems of parsley before blending all the solid ingredients for the marinade in a food processor. Place this blend in a large dish, and thin it with vinegar and wine. Cut the chicken into serving pieces of approximately equal size, scoring the skin here and there. Season with the salt and pepper. Coat the chicken in the marinade, moisten with a bit of olive oil and let it sit in a cold place for an hour, turning the pieces over 3 or 4 times.

In a hermetically sealed freezer bag (if none are available, use an ordinary plastic bag), mix the flour, salt, pepper, ginger, oregano and paprika. Drain the pieces of chicken, shaking well to remove the excess marinade. Put a few chicken pieces in the bag, close it tightly and shake until the pieces are well coated with the breading. Place the coated pieces of chicken on a grill so that they aren't touching each other, and let the coating set for 20 minutes.

Heat the oil in two deep frying pans. When the oil is very hot, add the pieces of chicken, again so that they aren't touching. Brown them quickly; then lower the heat, half-cover the pan and cook them gently over medium heat. Turn the pieces over once or twice during cooking. After 30 minutes, remove the cover and brown the chicken on all sides over high heat until it is nice and crispy. Place the chicken on several layers of paper towelling to absorb the excess oil before arranging it nicely on a serving dish. Decorate with lemon quarters and chopped parsley.

Liégoise Soup

*Mettez du lait dans un pot ou dans une poêle, avec du beurre ou de l'huile; ajoutez-y des
gousses d'ail pelées et pilées, du poivre, du sel et d'autres épices; détrempez aussi une
poignée de farine, plus ou moins, selon la grandeur du potage, et qu'elle soit remise au
four, ou dans une poêle, la retournant souvent avec un peu de lait ou du vin; faites
bouillir tout ensemble un peu de temps, remuez-le et versez-le sur des soupes de pain.*

La Varenne, Le Cuisinier françois, 1651

Whether meat or vegetable-based, in Louis XIV's time, "potages" were dishes cooked in a deep
pot. The transposition that we propose of this garlic-and-milk soup that La Varenne used to
moisten slices of bread is not unlike modern soups, and is similar to tourin.

SERVES 6

10 cloves garlic
40 g/ ⅙ cup butter
1.5 l/1.5 quarts milk
1 Tbsp. flour
300 g/ ⅔ lb. farmhouse bread
salt and pepper to taste
2 egg yolks (optional)

Peel and crush the garlic. Sauté it quickly in the melted butter in a
large cooking pot, without letting it brown. Leave it over low heat,
and sprinkle with flour, then moisten with a glass of water. As soon
as the mixture has become homogenous, pour the milk in, stirring
constantly. Salt and pepper to taste, bring to the boil, then let it simmer
for 20 minutes, making sure to keep an eye on it. If possible, just
before serving, add the two egg yolks, which you will have thinned
out first with a bit of water. Serve the hot soup over slices of lightly
toasted bread.

*F*ilet of Fatted Hen

SERVES 6

1 1.2-kg./3-lb. fatted hen
(Cornish Hen or similar)

100 g/ ¼ lb. bard of bacon
or lard

1 shallot

1 lemon

2 cloves garlic

2 Tbsp. capers

1 bunch flat-leaf parsley

1 bunch chives

1 bunch chervil

15 cl/ ½ cup olive oil

2 Tbsp. vinegar

salt & pepper to taste

Pre-heat the oven to high (220°C/420° F./Gas Mark 7). Season the bird all over with the salt and pepper and wrap it in the bard, which should be held in place with cooking string. Place it on a greased baking dish and roast for 1 hour, basting regularly with the cooking juices.

While the chicken is roasting, wash and spin or pat dry the herbs, peel the shallot and garlic and chop everything together finely in a food processor or spice blender. Pour the herb blend into a small bowl, add the olive oil, lemon juice, vinegar and capers. Season with the salt and pepper and leave in a cool place. Cool the cooked bird, then remove the flesh and cut it into strips. Don't forget the "sot-l'y-laisse" (literally, the "fools leave it", sometimes called the "oyster," a small tender piece at the bottom of the bird) of which Louis XIV is said to have been inordinately fond.

Arrange the strips of chicken in a single layer in a large serving dish. Pour the prepared sauce over it, as well as an extra splash of olive oil. Leave in a cool place to marinate until serving.

*V*eal Poupeline

*Hachez rouelle de veau avec graisse et un peu de lard, fines herbes, jaunes d'œufs crus,
sel, poivre, muscade et en faites un lit au fond d'une tourtière. Mettez ris de veau,
champignons par morceaux, truffes, crêtes, et la couvrer de la même chair hachée
comme une tourte; mettez un paquet par dehors. Quand vous voudrez servir, liez avec
jaunes d'œufs et jus de citron et par tranche.*

Pierre de Lune, Le Cuisinier, 1656

In Louis XIV's time, all sorts of pâtés were much appreciated. Pierre de Lune proposes this one
with veal. It must be baked in a slow oven.

SERVE 6

300 g / ⅔ lb. veal
200 g / 4/10 lb. raw lard
250 g / ½ lb. mushrooms
2 shallots, finely chopped
2 egg yolks
1 bunch parsley
1 bunch chives
1 bouquet garni (chives, thyme, bay leaf)
salt & pepper to taste

Melt the lard gently; chop the veal and mushrooms and mix them with
the lard. Add the finely chopped shallots, as well as chopped parsley
and chives to taste.

Thicken with the egg yolks; season with the salt and pepper. Pat the
mixture firmly into a rectangular terrine (a deep earthenware dish) or
a loaf pan, top it with the bouquet garni and cover with aluminium foil.

Place this dish in a larger one with water in it, to create a bain-marie
(double boiler) and bake in a slow oven (150°C/300° F./Gas mark 2)
for 1½ hours. Let the poupeline cool completely before attempting to
remove it from the dish, then slice and serve.

*A "poupelin," which in cookery
terms is a cake baked in the oven
and moistened with melted butter
after baking, originally meant a
new-born baby or a little doll.*

Meat, Fish

&

Poultry

French Beef Stew

Battez-le bien, lardez-le de gros lard, passez-le à la poêle et mettez-le dans une terrine avec un verre de vin blanc, 2 verres d'eau, un paquet garni, sel, poivre, laurier, citron vert, demi-douzaine de champignons et le bouchez bien dans une autre terrine avec de la pâte et faites cuire à petit feu. Quand il sera cuit, passez de la farine à la poêle avec du lard fondu et mettez dans votre terrine avec un jus de citron.

Pierre de Lune, Le Cuisinier, 1656

Did you know that we owe this classic French dish to Pierre de Lune?

SERVES 6

1.2 kg / 3 lb. rumpsteak

100 g/ ¼ lb. unsmoked bacon

2 large carrots

20 small, fresh onions

6 large mushrooms

juice of 1 lemon

25 cl/ 1 cup dry white wine

50 cl/ 2 cups water or beef bouillon

1 bouquet garni

salt & pepper to taste

FOR THE ROUX

20 g/ 1½ Tbsp. butter

1 Tbsp. flour

Cut the beef into chunks of about 5 cm./2 inches on each side. Heat the bacon in a stew pot, then add the beef and brown it on all sides. Moisten with the white wine; allow about half of it to evaporate before adding the water or bouillon, the bouquet garni and the mushrooms. Add salt and pepper to taste, cover and cook for about 2 hours on very low heat, stirring from time to time.

While the beef is stewing, peel the onions and carrots. Cut the carrots into thick slices, but leave the onions whole. After 2 hours, add the carrots and onions to the pot. Let everything stew, covered and at low heat, for 2 hours more.

When the cooking time is over, skim off any excess fat floating at the surface, then take a half cup of cooking juices.

In a saucepan, make a roux: melt the butter, add the flour, stirring constantly. When this paste begins to brown, add the half-cup of cooking juices and let everything thicken for 2 minutes. Pour your roux back into the stew pot, squeeze the juice of one lemon over it, and serve immediately.

Duck with Oysters

Votre canard étant cuit à la braise, vous passez 2 ou 3 champignons et 2 ou 3 truffes
avec un peu de lard fondu et les mouillez de jus de canard; étant cuits vous les liez d'un
bon coulis de veau et de jambon. Un moment avant de servir vous avez des huîtres; étant
ouvertes vous les mettez dans un plat et les laissez dans leur eau et les mettez sur un
fourneau. Faire 2 ou 3 tours; et sur-le-champ les étirez et les nettoyez l'une après l'autre
et les jetez dans votre ragoût et remettez le ragoût un peu sur le feu. Vous dresserez
votre canard sur le plat et jetez votre ragoût par-dessus et servez chaudement. Il faut
observer que l'huître ne veut point bouillir à cause qu'elle se racornit.

Massialot, Le Cuisinier roïal et bourgeois, 1691

Duck and oysters: an unexpectedly elegant combination.

SERVES 6

1 2-kg /4½-lb. duckling

18 oysters

200 g / ½-lb. chanterelle mushrooms

25 cl /1 cup dry white wine

10 cl / ½ cup heavy veal stock

10 g / ¾ Tbsp. butter

2 Tbsp. olive oil

1 onion

2 cloves garlic

1 bouquet garni (thyme, parsley, bay leaf)

1 stick cinnamon

3 cloves

Lightly season the duckling all over (inside and out) with the salt and pepper. Brown it on all sides in a large stew pot: this will take at least 10 minutes. When the duck is nicely browned, place it in a large dish and set aside. Pour all the grease out of the pot, wipe it clean and heat the olive oil on low heat. Soften the peeled, roughly chopped onion in the olive oil. Add the crushed garlic, bouquet garni, cinnamon stick and cloves. Put the whole duck back into the stew pot. Moisten with the white wine, cover and simmer over medium heat for 1½ hours, turning the bird every half hour. Once it's cooked, keep it warm in the oven while you prepare the sauce.

If need be, remove the excess grease from the stew pot before putting in the carefully cleaned mushrooms. Add the veal stock and bring to the boil. Cook over medium heat for 15 minutes. While the mushrooms are cooking, shuck the oysters. Discard the shells with their water, keeping only the oyster meat in a bowl in the refrigerator. Cut the duck up into serving pieces and place them on a serving dish. At the last possible moment, add the oysters to the sauce. Turn the heat off after a few seconds, cover and let the sauce rest for 3 minutes. Remove the bouquet garni and the cinnamon stick, adjust the seasoning if need be. Pour the sauce over the duck and decorate the dish with a bit of parsley.

Our Tip

Be very careful with the seasoning: this dish requires very little salt. The veal stock and the oyster juice generally provide quite a bit of salt. So don't salt the sauce until all the ingredients are in, or simply provide a small dish of "fleur de sel de Guérande" (flower of Breton sea salt) on the table.

Barbary Duck with Prune Wine

Potage de canard à l'arabesque, Pierre de Lune, Le Cuisinier, 1656

Barbary Duck, (also known as Musk or Muscovy Duck), native to South and Central America, was first seen in France in the 16th century. Its unusual shape has been little changed by breeding. On the other hand, the domesticated birds are often white, while the wild birds have a brownish-black plumage with green highlights. Very different from the mallard duck, it is sometimes called the mute duck, as opposed to the noisy mallard…

SERVES 6

3 500-g/1-lb Barbary duck breast fillets

50 g/1.75 oz. lard

4 turnips

1 medium onion

1 clove garlic

10 prunes (preferably from Agen)

30 cl/1 ¼ cup white wine

10 cl/ ½ cup poultry bouillon

1 Tbsp. capers

20 pitted olives

1 bouquet garni

5 cloves

1 cinnamon stick

juice of 1 orange

salt & pepper to taste

Make three deep incisions on the skin side of each duck breast. In a stew pot, melt half the lard and brown the duck breasts on both sides, starting with the skin side first. While the breasts are browning, heat the white wine with the cinnamon in a small saucepan. Add the prunes and simmer over very low heat. Peel and mince the onion and garlic. Peel and dice the turnips.

Remove the duck breasts from the stew pot, and keep them warm on a serving dish. Throw out the fat in which they cooked. Melt the rest of the lard in the same pot and soften the onion for a few minutes. Add the turnips, the garlic, the cloves and the bouquet garni. Let everything stew for a few minutes before putting the duck breasts in, after having first seasoned them with salt and pepper; then add the olives. Strain the prune wine through a bit of muslin (cheesecloth).

Moisten the dish with the bouillon and the mulled wine. Let it cook for 30 minutes over medium heat. Towards the end of the cooking time, add the capers and adjust the seasoning as necessary. Cut the duck breasts into thin strips that you will present in their "soup." Just before serving, squeeze the juice of an orange over the dish.

$\mathcal{S}$tuffed Carp

Écaillez la carpe et la dépouillez par le dos, que la peau reste entière. Hachez bien la chair, assaisonnez de sel, poivre, muscade, fines herbes, ciboulette et beurre. Farcissez la peau avec ladite chair, champignons, laitance de carpe, huîtres, culs d'artichauts cuits, 2 clous de girofle. Assemblez le tout comme si la carpe était entière. Dressez un pâté de la longueur de la carpe en pâte fine, puis couvrez-le et faites-le cuire à petit feu. En servant, mettez-y un bon morceau de beurre et un jus de citron.

Pierre de Lune, Le Cuisinier, 1656

Saltwater fish being rare, 17th-century cooks were more familiar with freshwater ones, and carp appeared on many menus. Its taste, which our modern palates are less familiar with, goes very well with unusual stuffings, like this one, suggested by Pierre de Lune.

SERVES 6

1 2-kg/ 4½-lb. carp

6 fresh oysters

1 shallot

1 clove garlic

100 g/ ¼ lb. cultivated mushrooms

40 g/3 Tbsp. butter

2 cooked artichoke hearts

25 cl/1 cup white wine

a few sprigs flat-leaf parsley

1 bouquet chives

1 branch thyme

1 lemon for juice

1 clove

a pinch of nutmeg

Ask your fishmonger to prepare the carp for stuffing (i.e. gut it and remove the "backbone", but without cutting all the way through). Ask him to take care to remove and set aside the milt, which you will need. Preheat the oven to 200 °C/400° F/Gas Mark 6. Wash and chop the parsley and chives; rub the needles off the branch of thyme. Finely chop the peeled shallot and garlic, the cleaned mushrooms and the clove. Incorporate the carp milt cut into chunks, the artichoke hearts, the oysters and half the butter. Chop quickly in the blender or food processor. Add the herbs and nutmeg. Season with salt and pepper.

Place the carp on a large greased baking dish. Season the inside with salt and pepper, then stuff it with the mushroom mixture. Sew the cavity closed with a large needle and cooking thread. Lightly salt the outside, moisten with the white wine, dot with 2 Tbsp. of butter and bake for one hour. Baste frequently with the cooking juices.

Present the fish whole in the baking dish, accompanied by a sauce made from the cooking juices to which you have added 1 Tbsp. of butter and some fresh lemon juice.

*V*enison Civet (Stew)

Pierre de Lune, Le Cuisinier, 1656

SERVES 6

1.2 kg./3 lb. shoulder of deer

50 g/2 oz. lard

75 cl/3 cups white wine

2 onions

2 cloves garlic

1 bouquet garni (thyme, parsley, scallion, bay leaf)

2 cloves

1 pinch nutmeg

1 lump sugar

20 g.1 ½ Tbsp. butter

2 Tbsp. flour

1 pinch Cayenne pepper (optional)

Pierre de Lune specifies that doe, stag, or "any other venison" can be accommodated in this manner.

Peel and dice the onion and garlic. Cut the venison into chunks about 5 cm/2 inches on each side. In a deep frying pan, melt the lard and brown the venison chunks on all sides. Add the onion and garlic, mix well, and keep cooking over low heat.

In a saucepan, bring the wine to a boil and let it reduce for a few minutes. Flambé it to get rid of the excess alcohol. Pour this reduction into the frying pan and let it simmer over low heat for 45 minutes. Season with salt and pepper, add the spices (bouquet garni, nutmeg, Cayenne pepper, cloves) and sugar.

Cook gently for 2 hours. If the sauce is too runny, thicken it with a quick roux: melt the butter and add the flour. Stir and cook for a moment, then moisten with a ladleful of the cooking juices. Let it boil for 2-3 minutes before pouring back into the pan. Mix carefully and extend the cooking as necessary to allow the sauce to thicken. Before serving, adjust the seasoning if necessary.

Salmon Steaks in White Sauce

Quand l'anguille sera écorchée, mettez-la en tranches, passez-la à la poêle au beurre;
assaisonnez de sel, de poivre, clous de girofle, une feuille de laurier, un verre de vin
blanc, muscade. Quand l'anguille sera cuite, faites une sauce blanche avec des jaunes
d'œufs et du verjus. Garnissez avec des tranches de citron et des croûtons frits.

Pierre de Lune, Le Cuisinier, 1656

In 1656, Pierre de Lune composed a recipe to accommodate eel slices in sauce. Eel has become very rare on our present-day markets. Only the transparent-spaghetti like baby eels, known as civelles or pibales, are still eaten in some regional dishes. Eel can be replaced here with salmon steaks, as salmon is also fatty. And to accompany this delicate dish, do consider preparing La Varenne Aspargus Ragout (in the Side Dish chapter).

SERVES 6

6 salmon steaks
60 g/ ½ cup butter
fish stock
30 g/ ⅓ cup flour
2 egg yolks
15 cl/ ½ cup dry white wine
juice of ½ lemon
3 cloves
1 bay leaf
3 pinches nutmeg
salt & pepper to taste

FOR THE GARNISH
2 lemons
a few sprigs parsley
fried croutons

Sauté the salmon steaks in 30 g/¼ cup hot butter, with salt, pepper, cloves, bay leaf, 10 cl/two-thirds of the white wine and the nutmeg.

While the fish is cooking, prepare the sauce: melt the rest of the butter over low heat, add the flour and stir well, moisten with the fish stock and the remaining 5 cl/ one third of the wine. Let it simmer gently, stirring constantly. Season with salt and pepper, and when it's sufficiently cooked, thicken with the two egg yolks and add the juice of ½ lemon.

Arrange the cooked salmon steaks in a deep serving dish, pour the sauce on top and garnish with lemon slices, chopped parsley and croutons.

Our Tip

It is quite difficult to give the precise amount of liquid necessary for making white sauce: it depends on the quality of the flour. Stop adding fish stock when the sauce has acquired the desired consistency.

Rather than making your own fish stock, you can use a reconstituted, powdered stock.

Marinated Veal Liver

Coupez le foie par tranches et le mettez au vinaigre, sel, poivre, un paquet ; farinez et le faites frire en lard fondu, et servez avec persil, poivre blanc et vinaigre à l'ail.

Pierre de Lune, Le Cuisinier, 1656

SERVES 6

6 150-g/ ⅓-lb slices veal liver
100 g/ ¼ lb lard
100 g/ ⅔ cup flour
1 bouquet garni (thyme, parsley, bay leaf and chives)
2 cloves
2 cloves garlic
20 cl/ ⅘ cup vinegar

FOR THE GARNISH
A few sprigs flat-leaf parsley
chervil

Season both sides of each slice of liver with salt and pepper, then place them in a single layer in a large dish. Pour over the vinegar, add the bouquet garni and let it marinate for 20 minutes in a cool place. While the liver is marinating, peel and finely chop the garlic and the parsley separately. Drain the liver slices and lightly dredge them in flour. Melt the lard in one, or if need be, two pans; brown the liver on high heat for 5 minutes on each side.

Keep the liver warm on a serving plate. Sauté the garlic in the pan, but without letting it brown. Deglaze the pan with a bit of vinegar, top with the chopped parsley and reduce for a moment.

Pour this sauce over the hot slices of liver. Garnish with chervil before serving.

Gras Fritters

After blanching the foies, if they are too plump, cut them into two or three pieces, which you will dip in a normal fritter batter, except without any flower-blossom water flavouring. Fry until the batter is nicely dry and browned, garnish with flowers, lemon and pomegranate, and serve with orange or lemon juice.

L'Art de bien traiter, 1664

 Rabbit Stew

SERVES 6

1 1.2-kg/3-lb. rabbit
50 g/ 3 ½ Tbsp. lard
20 cl/1 cup white wine
2 cl/ 1 cup chicken bouillon
1 large onion
1 clove garlic
1 bouquet garni (thyme,
parsley, chive, bay leaf)
1 Tbsp. flour
juice of one orange
salt & pepper to taste

FOR THE GARNISH

1 orange
a few sprigs flat-leaf parsley

Cut the rabbit into pieces and brown them in a stew pot with the melted lard. Sprinkle them lightly with flour, salt and pepper, then add the diced onion and garlic. When everything's nicely browned, moisten with the white wine and the bouillon. Add the bouquet garni and cook over medium heat for 40 minutes.

Pour in the fresh orange juice and let everything simmer gently for another 15 minutes. Before serving, adjust the seasoning and garnish with chopped parsley and thick slices of orange.

Fresh Mackerel Stew

L.S.R. L'Art de bien traiter, 1674

SERVES 6

6 gutted 250 g/ ½-lb. mackerel

35 cl/ 1 ⅓ cups white Bordeaux

20 g/ 1 ½ Tbsp. butter

1 tsp. vinegar

2 Tbsp. crème fraîche / sour cream

1 orange

2 shallots

2 cloves garlic

1 heaping spoonful capers

a few sprigs flat-leaf parsley

1 bunch fresh chives

1 bay leaf

20 or so green grapes (optional)

salt & pepper to taste

Peel and finely chop the shallots and garlic. Chop the chives, but leave a few blades whole. In a deep pot, melt the butter and sauté the shallots over low heat for 3 minutes. Then add the garlic, parsley, chives and bay leaf. Wash the mackerel and cut each one into 2 pieces. Season with salt and pepper, and place them in the pot. Pour in the wine and vinegar, and let it come to a gentle boil.

While the mackerel are cooking, peel the orange right to the pulp (don't leave any white pith), then slice it thinly. Add the orange slices to the pot, cover and cook over medium heat for 10 minutes more.

Arrange the pieces of mackerel in a serving dish and strain the bouillon through a bit of muslin (cheesecloth). Pour this sauce into the pot, add the grapes and reduce over high heat for 5 minutes. Whisk in the crème fraîche (sour cream) and adjust the seasoning if need be. Top the pieces of fish with this sauce, and garnish with capers and freshly cut chives.

Leg of Mutton with Oysters

Il faut une épaule de mouton bien mortifiée ; la larder de gros lard, assaisonner de sel, poivre, muscade, ciboulette, et la faire cuire à la broche ; l'arroser d'eau et un peu de sel ; quand elle sera cuite, mettre dans la sauce huîtres, anchois, câpres, champignons ; passer en poêle avec lard fondu et farine ; servir l'épaule dans la sauce avec tranche de citron.

Pierre de Lune, Le Cuisinier, 1656

SERVES 6

1.5 kg/ 3-⅓ lb. shoulder of lamb
1 tsp. grated nutmeg
1 bunch fresh chives
15l ½ cup water
1 lemon

FOR THE SAUCE

250 g / ½ lb small cultivated mushrooms
12 oysters
2 anchovies packed in oil
1 shallot
1 Tbsp. capers
1 Tbsp. oil
20 g/1 ½ Tbsp. butter

Ask the butcher to prepare the shoulder of lamb (i.e. to bone it, lard it and tie it up for roasting), setting aside the bones cut into chunks. Preheat the oven to 220°C/425° F/Gas Mark 7. Season the lamb with the salt and pepper and rub it with the nutmeg and the finely chopped chives. If your oven has a spit, roast the meat on it for 45 minutes, putting the bones to roast in the dripping pan (broiling pan) with a bit of water. Otherwise, simply place your lamb in a lightly greased baking dish, surround it with the bones and oven roast everything. After about 20 minutes, turn the meat over, and let it cook for 15 minutes more. Moisten the dish with a glass of water and let it boil for 10 minutes more. Keep the meat warm, recuperate the cooking juices and strain them through a piece of muslin (cheesecloth).

In a pan, prepare the sauce by sautéing the shallot in butter and oil. Clean the mushrooms and, if they're big, slice them thickly. Add them to the pan and soften them over very low heat for 10 minutes. Shuck the oysters, throw away the liquid in the shell, and put the oyster meat in a bowl in a cool place. When the mushrooms have rejected all their water, add the anchovies cut into pieces and sauté quickly. The mixture should brown nicely. Moisten with the meat cooking juices and let it come back to the boil. Add the capers, then the oysters and the juices in the bowl. Let it all simmer for a minute.

Slice the meat, arrange it on a serving dish and top each slice with a few spoonfuls of the sauce. Garnish with lemon slices and serve the rest of the sauce in a sauceboat.

Hot Pheasant or Duck Pâté

Prenez de la chair de faisan et de la chair de poularde et un morceau de cuisse de veau tendre: hachez bien le tout ensemble, avec du persil, de la ciboule, des champignons, des mousserons, quelques ris de veau, du jambon cuit et du lard cru. Étant bien haché et assaisonné de fines herbes et épices, sel, poivre, formez-en un bon godiveau et faites une pâte un peu forte. Si vous voulez, vous en ferez un pâté à 2 abaisses, ou seulement avec une. Vous ferez bien cuire votre pâté et voulant servir, vous le dégraisserez et y mettrez un coulis de champignons. Servez chaudement.

Massialot, Le Cuisinier roïal et bourgeois, 1691

Massialot proposes this recipe for pheasant or young fatted hen. To make it easier to do at any time of year, you could use duck or even chicken. As a main dish, serve with a nice salad with garlic.

SERVES 6

300 g/ ⅔ lb. puff/flaky (croissant-type) pastry

200 g/ ½ lb. duck breast filet

200 g/ ½ lb chicken

200 g/ ½ lb tender veal (eye, topside (top round) etc.)

150 g/ ⅓ lb. ham

150 g / ⅓ lb. unsmoked bacon

250 g / ½ lb. mushrooms

20 g / 1 ½ Tbsp. butter

1 egg yolk

1 bunch chives

a few sprigs parsley

salt & pepper to taste

Chop all the meats together with the mushrooms and herbs. Mix well to obtain a homogenous blend, season generously with pepper.

Preheat the oven to 180°C/350° F/Gas Mark 4. On a floured work surface, roll out three quarters of the pastry dough, and cover the bottom of a large, high-sided earthenware terrine (paté dish), allowing 3 cm/an inch of dough to hang over the edge all around. Roll out the rest of the dough to make a top crust. Fill the crust with the meat-and-mushroom mixture and cover with the rest of the dough, sealing the edges together with a fork or with your fingers. Cut a small opening into the centre of the top crust, and insert a small cardboard "chimney" to allow steam to escape. Brush the surface with an egg yolk thinned with a tablespoon of water.

Bake for 1½ hours. Check on it a few times during baking, and when the top crust begins to brown, loosely cover it with aluminium foil. Now follow the maître cuisinier's advice: "You should bake your pâté well, and, when it is ready, serve it with puréed mushrooms."

*Y*oung Squab Italian Style

Il faut les fendre par-dessus le dos, les faire tremper dans de l'huile d'olive, sel, poivre, laurier, un paquet, un peu de vinaigre ; leur faire une pâte bien claire et les passer dans la pâte, puis les faire frire dans la même huile et les servir au vinaigre rosat, ou à l'ail avec cresson amorti dans le sel et le vinaigre

Pierre de Lune, Le cuisinier, 1656

SERVES 6

3 squab
25 g/2 Tbsp. butter
2 tp 3 Tbsp. breadcrumbs
FOR THE MARINADE
25 cl/1 cup olive oil
1 bunch flat-leaf parsley
3 sprigs thyme
2 branches rosemary
1 bay leaf
1 Tbsp. vinegar
FOR THE SIDE DISH
1 bunch watercress
3 Tbsp. olive oil
2 Tbsp. balsamic vinegar
salt & pepper to taste

Prepare the marinade: wash the herbs and chop them in the blender or herb chopper. Spread them into the bottom of a large dish, and pour the oil and vinegar over them. Split the squab's backs open, but leave the stomachs intact. Flatten them with the palm of your hand, brush them all over with the marinade. If need be, drizzle a bit more olive oil over them; season with the salt and pepper. Let them marinate in a cool place for an hour.

Melt the butter in a large pan. Drain the excess marinade off the squab, keeping the marinade in the dish, and brown the squab gently over low heat for 15 minutes. Let them cool before dredging them in the leftover marinade and then in breadcrumbs. Grill them in the oven (in the middle of the oven, not too close to the grill), for 30 minutes, turning once.

While the squab is cooking, clean the watercress carefully, removing the thick stems and any yellowed leaves. Wash the cress twice, changing the water; drain dry and put in a large salad bowl. Just before serving, drizzle generously with olive oil and balsamic vinegar. Season with salt and pepper to taste, toss and present as a side dish for the squab, which should be served cut into four pieces each.

ish Stew

La Varenne, Le Cuisinier françois, 1656

 As Varenne specifies, any whole fish works for this recipe from Le Cuisinier françois. Impress your guests by preparing large fish (turbot, John Dory, bass or salmon) or adapt it to smaller ones, like red mullet, salmon trout or sea bream.

SERVES 6

1 1.5-kg/3½-lb. whole bass

25 cl/1 cup dry white wine

30 g/2 Tbsp butter

5 cloves

1 orange

1 bay leaf

2 slices stale farmhouse bread or 2 Tbsp. breadcrumbs

1 pinch grated nutmeg

a few sprigs fresh chervil

salt & pepper to taste

Ask your fishmonger to gut and scale the whole bass. Before you start preparing the fish, remember to preheat your oven to (250°C/500° F./Gas Mark 10). Wash the fish and lay it in a large baking dish. Spread ⅔ of the butter over the bass, season generously with salt and pepper inside and out. Moisten with the white wine, then add the nutmeg, cloves and bay leaf. With a vegetable peeler, peel off the orange peel, being careful not to take the white pith. Cut the zest into thin strips, and add them to the dish.

Lower the oven to (190° C/380° F./Gas Mark 5) and bake for 45 minutes. In the meantime, toast the bread and crush it or spin it though the blender to reduce it to crumbs. Remove the dish from the oven and turn on the grill. Sprinkle the breadcrumbs over the fish and top with the last bit of butter. Grill the bass until it is nicely brown, about 3 minutes.

Garnish with the chervil and serve immediately

*P*artridge & Cabbage Potage

Lardez les perdrix de moyen lard ; les passez à la poêle avec lard ; les mettez cuire avec bouillon de bœuf ; assaisonnez d'un paquet, sel, poivre ; passez les choux après les avoir fait blanchir dans l'eau, et hachez bien menu à la réserve de quelque pomme pour garnir ; mettez moelle de bœuf, garnissez de saucisson de Boulogne par tranches, jus de mouton et de champignons.

Pierre de Lune, Le cuisinier, 1656

SERVES 6

2 cleaned and barded partridge

1 Milanese cabbage

1 cervelas

100 g/ ¼ pound lard

100 g / ¼ pound cubed bacon

1 litre/1 quart beef bouillon

1 bouquet garni (thyme, parsley, bay leaf, chives)

4 cloves

1 pinch nutmeg

1 large onion

a few sprigs chervil

salt & pepper to taste

Remove the old outer leaves from the cabbage, cut it in quarters and blanch it in salted water for 15 minutes. Drain it, and press hard to eliminate as much liquid as possible. While the cabbage is blanching, melt the lard in a large pot and brown the whole partridges on all sides. Add the bacon, the whole cervelas sausage and the onion stuck with the cloves.

Cover and cook for 15 minutes. Add the blanched, drained cabbage and cook, uncovered, for 10 minutes to evaporate the excess liquid. Season lightly with salt, and sprinkle with the nutmeg. Moisten with the hot bouillon, add the bouquet garni and simmer over low heat for 2 hours, or until the meat is tender.

In a serving dish, arrange the cabbage around the quartered partridges; garnish with peeled slices of cervelas sausage. If need be, reduce the cooking juices over high heat until you have about the equivalent of a cup of sauce.

Just before serving, pour the sauce over the partridge and garnish with the chervil.

Chicken on Embers

Chapon à la braise, L'Escole parfaite des Officiers de bouche, 1662

This is an ideal dish for a picnic or a buffet, like Louis XIV enjoyed during his celebrated hunting parties. We'll bet that the capon that L'Escole parfaite des Officiers de bouche ("The Perfect School of Officers of the King's Table") suggests using for this recipe would react just like the one in the fable (see below).

SERVES 6

1 nice, plump free-range chicken (1½ kg/3½ lbs.)

100 g/¼ lb. unsmoked ham

1 strip of bard (approx. 80 g/ ⅙ lb.)

FOR THE MARINADE

5 Tbsp. olive oil

1 large shallot

1 bunch scallions

a few sprigs flat-leaf parsley

3 sprigs thyme

1 branch rosemary

2 large cloves garlic

salt & pepper to taste

"Capons do not give us their confidence,
Whether from instinct, or from experience,
This one, though it had been hard to clutch,
Was meant the next day to be part of a grand lunch,
Beautifully presented in a large dish,
An honour, yet one with which,
The bird would have preferred to dispense."

(Jean de La Fontaine, Fables, Book VIII, The Falcon and The Capon.)

Split the bird's back in two. Make slight incisions at the articulations (top of the thighs and wings), without separating them from the rest of the bird. Press the whole thing firmly with the palm of your hand so that it lies flat. Grease the bottom of a baking dish with the bard before placing the chicken in the dish.

Using a blender or an electric herb chopper, finely chop the rinsed parsley, the peeled shallot and garlic, and the thyme and rosemary needles. Add the olive oil to the herbs, season generously with the salt and pepper. Brush both sides of the bird with this mixture. Sprinkle the diced ham over the bird, cover with a sheet of aluminium foil and place in the refrigerator for a few hours. Preheat the oven to (175°C/350° F./Gas Mark ¾). Roast for an hour, basting frequently with the cooking juices. Turn the chicken once, and, if need be, moisten with a few spoonfuls of white wine or water during the roasting. After an hour, remove the aluminium foil, light the grill and brown the chicken for a few minutes. Let it sit for 5 minutes before carving into serving pieces. Can be eaten hot or cold, with peas with bacon or asparagus in a mild vinaigrette.

Our Tip

This recipe can be done just as well on a barbecue on a warm summer evening.

Chicken with Champagne & Olives

Il faut avoir des poulardes bien tendres, bien retroussées, et les faire rôtir, une bonne barde de lard sur l'estomac. Durant qu'elles cuisent, faites le ragoût composé d'un petit brin de persil et de ciboule hachée et passez avec un peu de lard et de farine. Étant passé, mettez-y 2 cuillerées de jus et un verre de vin de Champagne, des câpres hachées, un anchois, des olives écrasées, une goutte d'huile d'olive, un bouquet de fines herbes. Pour lier la sauce, ajoutez-y un bon coulis, le tout bien assaisonné et bien dégraissé. Prenez les poulardes rôties et ayant coupé les jambes à la jointure et ficelé aux ailes, aux cuisses et à l'estomac, écrasez-les un peu et les mettez ensuite dans la sauce. Un peu auparavant que de servir, pressez-y un jus d'orange et servez chaudement.

Massialot, Le Cuisinier roïal et bourgeois, 1691

A bourgeois dish or a royal one? Massialot couldn't decide, proposing a refined recipe for Fatted Hen with Olives, which we present here, for a "a taste fest".

SERVES 6

1 1 ½-kg/3½-lb. free-range hen

1 strip of bard

25 cl/1 cup champagne or blanc de blancs demi-sec

50 cl d'eau/2 cups water or chicken bouillon

1 chopped shallot

2 Tbsp. olive oil

25 pitted green olives

2 Tbsp. capers

juice of ½ lemon

juice of 1 orange

2 well-rinsed, chopped anchovies

1 bouquet garni (chives, flat-leaf parsley, thyme and bay leaf)

a few sprigs fresh chervil (optional)

salt & pepper to taste

Preheat the oven (180°C/350° F./Gas Mark 4), place the chicken in a large baking dish; season generously with salt and pepper. Cover the chicken breast with the bard, which you should hold in place with cooking string. Raise the oven temperature to 230°C/450° F./Gas Mark 8) and roast for 30 minutes. Turn the chicken over and continue cooking for another 30 minutes or so. Lower the oven temperature if necessary. While the bird is roasting, gently cook the shallot in the olive oil in a large stew pot. Add the anchovies. Let them cook for a few minutes. Pour in the champagne and the lemon juice and bring to the boil. Add the bouquet garni, capers, olives and the water or bouillon, and let it simmer over low heat.

When the chicken is cooked, let it cool for 5 minutes on a carving board (outside of the oven). Throw away most of the grease at the bottom of the roasting pan, but carefully recuperate the dark brown drippings that should be added to the champagne sauce in the pot. Carve the chicken into serving pieces and place them in the sauce. Let everything simmer together over low heat for 15 minutes. Just before serving, remove the bouquet garni, squeeze the orange juice over and garnish with chopped chervil or parsley.

Our Tip

A fatted hen is a young hen that is being fatted for the table rather than kept for laying. With its meltingly tender, tasty flesh, it is perfect for roasting over the holidays. During the last 3 weeks before butchering, skim milk should be added to the hen's diet, giving the flesh an incomparably fine, mellow texture. This rare and costly bird can be replaced with a nice plump free-range hen.

_H_ow to make a "miroton"

Massialot, Le Cuisinier roïal et bourgeois, 1691

Cooks, as people with a sense of economic responsibility, have always looked for appetising ways to use up leftovers. Massialot, who was interested in both bourgeois tables and royal ones, proposed preparing a "miroton". Using mushrooms, truffles and lard, where modern cooks would tend to use onions and butter or oil, he granted leftover boiled beef a sense of noblesse, thereby creating one of the first classics of bistro cuisine.

SERVES 6

900 g/2 lb. leftover boiled beef (from a pot-au-feu, for example)

3 large onions

200 g/ ½ lb cooked ham

75 g/5 Tbsp. butter (or 30 g/2 Tbsp. butter and 1 Tbsp. oil)

2 Tbsp. flour

2 Tbsp. red-wine vinegar

a few sprigs flat-leaf parsley

1 bunch chives

25 cl/1 cup beef bouillon

1 Tbsp. tomato paste

1 desalted anchovy (optional)

salt & pepper to taste

Peel the onions and chop them finely. Lightly brown them in a hot pan with the butter (or butter and oil blend). Add the diced ham. Sprinkle with the flour and mix well. Moisten with the vinegar, mix again, and pour in the bouillon in which you will have diluted the tomato paste. Add the finely chopped parsley and chives, season with salt and pepper. Let the sauce thicken for 15 to 20 minutes, stirring regularly. You can strengthen the taste by adding an anchovy (well-soaked to remove the saltiness) while the sauce is cooking and letting the anchovy dissolve into the sauce. Cut the beef into thin slices.

Melt some butter in a deep frying pan, and alternate slices of beef with the onion ragout. Adjust the seasoning if necessary, cover and simmer over low heat for 20 minutes.

It's up to you to decide if you wish to follow Massialot's final piece of advice: "Before serving, add the juice of one lemon and arrange your dish properly."

Marinated Tuna or Sole

SERVES 6

3 red-tuna steaks
1 untreated lemon
juice of 1 orange
1 shallot
2 bay leaves
1 bunch fresh chives
a few sprigs chervil
3 Tbsp. olive oil
oil for frying

Put your tuna steaks, seasoned with salt and pepper, into a frying pan with hot oil (the frying oil, not the olive oil). Fry the tuna for 4 minutes on each side. Place the fish steaks in a deep serving dish. In the same pan in which you fried the tuna, quickly sauté the peeled, chopped shallot; add the finely sliced lemon and the bay leaf. Let them cook together for a few minutes over medium heat. Add the orange juice, and pour the sauce over the fish. Drizzle olive oil over it and sprinkle with the chopped chives and chervil. Let the dish cool to room temperature before covering it with plastic wrap. Serve chilled.

Marinated Sole

As Pierre de Lune points out, this marinade can accompany several different types of fish. Try it with filets of sole, salmon steaks or even scallops, which you should flour lightly before frying.

$\mathcal{S}$callop Pie

L'Escole parfaite des Officiers de bouche ("The Perfect School of Officers of the King's Table")
proposed a recipe for "Carp Milt Pie". Milt from carp, mackerel or herring was a common
foodstuff, even though, in order to be used in cooking, the milt – sperm from a male fish which
could fecundate eggs laid by a female – required a fairly fastidious preparation process, including
rendering and blanching. It was then served as a side dish for meat or fish, along with
mushrooms and sauce, or prepared in an omelette.
Carp milt is hard to find nowadays; it can easily be replaced with scallops (sea or bay). The
original recipe called for both cultivated mushrooms and wild morel ones – which are fairly rare
on the market nowadays. Cultivated mushrooms only will do just fine.

SERVES 6

*FOR THE VOL-AU-VENT PASTRY
CASE*

*500 g/1 lb puff/flaky
(croissant-type) pastry
dough*
1 egg yolk

FOR THE FILLING
800 g/2 lb. scallops
250 g/ ½ lb. mushrooms
30 g/2 Tbsp. butter
20 cl/ ⅘ cup heavy cream
1 bunch fresh chives
a few sprigs flat-leaf parsley
1 pinch grated nutmeg
juice of 1 lemon
salt & pepper to taste

Prepare the vol-au-vent pastry case: on a floured board, roll out the
dough to about 2-cm/ ¾-inch thick and cut out a 25-cm-/10-inch-
wide circle. Brush it with the egg yolk thinned with a teaspoonful of
water. With the tip of a knife, make light incisions around the edge of
the circle. For the top crust, again with the tip of the knife, lightly trace
a second circle (without cutting all the way through the dough) an
inch inside the first. Draw a trellis pattern on the top crust. Place the
dough on a buttered baking tray and bake in the oven (200° C/400°
F./Gas Mark 6) for half an hour to 35 minutes.

While the pastry case is baking, prepare the mushrooms (first cut off
the sandy bit, then wash, dry and slice the mushrooms). Squeeze the
juice of one lemon over them to keep them from going brown. Rinse
the scallops. Melt the butter in a pan, and sauté the scallops and mushrooms for 7 or 8 minutes. Season with salt and pepper. Add the cream
and the chopped chives and parsley, mix gently and simmer over low
heat for 10 to 15 minutes until the cream makes a thick coating for
the scallops and mushrooms.

As soon as the vol-au-vent case is baked – the top should be nicely
brown – take it out of the oven, carefully remove the cover, and throw
away any white, doughy bits clogging the inside of the case. Place the
bottom of the case on a serving dish, fill it with the hot scallop filling,
place the cover on top and serve immediately.

Another recipe appeared in L'Escole parfaite des Officiers de bouche :
"Chopped Crayfish Pie."

After the crayfish have been shelled, chop them and thicken them with
carp milt, chopped mushrooms, pike liver, morel mushrooms, truffles,
salt & pepper, nutmeg, and a packet of herbs stuck with cloves, and
some good butter. Cover and cook. Top with lemon or orange juice
just before serving.

*M*incemeat Pie

Louis XIV's time was the golden age of light-as-air pastry cases, and the crisp, golden crusts of all sorts of sweet and savoury pies and pâtés contributed to the harmony of a well-furnished table. Variations on these themes were practically infinite, and Pierre de Lune was a master of the art of the pie crust.

Nowadays, success in these recipes is easy to achieve: ready-made pie crusts and dough, whether frozen or refrigerated, is a great help, and the results are worthy of a grand table.

SERVES 6

300 g/ ⅔ lb. puff/flaky (croissant-type) pastry dough

200 g/ ½ lb chicken meat

200 g/ ½ lb de tender veal

200 g/ ½ lb raw lard

200 g/ ½ lb artichoke hearts

300 g/ ⅔ lb. mushrooms

20 g/ 1½ Tbsp. butter

1 egg yolk

1 bunch chives

a few sprigs flat-leaf parsley

3 to 4 pinches nutmeg

salt & pepper to taste

Roll out the pastry dough on a well-floured work surface, making it big enough to cover the bottom and sides and make a top crust for a large pie dish. Butter the dish and line it with the pastry dough. Preheat the oven to 180°C/350° C./Gas Mark 4.

Prepare the filling: cut the sandy bit off of the bottom of the mushroom stems, then wash and dry the mushrooms. Melt the raw lard in a pan. Chop and mix the chicken, veal, lard, artichokes and mushrooms in the blender. Add the chopped herbs and nutmeg, season generously with salt and pepper. Make sure the mixture is fairly homogenous.

Fill the pie crust with this mixture, then close it with a top crust, into which you should cut a small hole in the centre to release steam. Brush the top with an egg yolk thinned with a tablespoon of water.

Bake for 1¼ hours. Keep an eye on the cooking: when the top crust begins to brown, cover it loosely with a sheet of aluminium foil.

Serve hot. As a side dish, you can prepare a purée of mushrooms and artichoke hearts.

Trout in Ham

SERVES 6

6 trout of 180 g/ ⅓- ½ lb. each, scaled and gutted

100 g/ ¼ lb lard

6 slices Bayonne (raw, salt-cured) ham

5 cl / ⅕ cup dry white wine

5 cl / ⅕ cup court bouillon

200 g / ½ lb. cultivated mushrooms

1 bouquet garni (thyme, parsley, chives, bay leaf)

1 pinch nutmeg

1 Tbsp. lemon juice

1 lime, quartered, for garnish

salt & pepper to taste

Wrap each trout in a slice of ham. Cook the fish in the melted lard for 5 minutes on each side. Moisten with the white wine and the court bouillon. Add the bouquet garni and the nutmeg, and let everything simmer together over low heat for 5 minutes.

While the fish is simmering, clean and chop the mushrooms and sauté them for a few minutes in butter. Add them to the pan with the fish, and reduce the sauce somewhat.

Before serving, pour the lemon juice over the fish, adjust the seasoning of the sauce if necessary and garnish with the quartered lime.

*T*urbot in court bouillon

L'Art de bien traiter, 1664

Serves 6

1 1.3-kg/3-lb. turbot, gutted
and scaled by the
fishmonger

25 cl/ cup white wine

1 lemon + 1 orange

For the marinade

10 cl/ ½ cup wine

juice of 1 lemon, 5 Tbsp. oil

2 Tbsp. wine vinegar

2 large onions, sliced

needles from 2 branches
thyme

needles from 1 branch
rosemary

1 bay leaf, 5 cloves

salt & pepper to taste

For the garnish

1 bunch curly parsley

1 lemon cut into sixths

two red roses, washed and
dried (optional)

two different vinaigrettes
(as desired)

Mix all of the marinade ingredients in a small bowl. Season the fish with salt and pepper, then place it in a large baking dish. Pour the marinade over and let it stand in the refrigerator.

After 15 minutes, turn the fish over, and put it back in the refrigerator. Preheat the oven to (190°C/380° F./Gas Mark 5). Peel the lemon and orange carefully, removing all the white pith, then cut them into thin slices. After the fish has marinated for another 15 minutes, take the dish out of the refrigerator, moisten the turbot with the 25 cl/ 1 cup of wine and lay the orange and lemon slices over the fish. Cover the dish with a sheet of aluminium foil and bake for an hour.

Take the fish out of the oven, and let it cool in its cooking juices for at least another hour before serving. For a stunningly festive dish, follow the author's advice: "Serve on a white tablecloth, garnished with lemon and flowers, with a profusion of parsley and two different vinaigrettes on either side."

Our Tip

Instead of vinaigrette, you could simply use the cooking juices, strained through muslin (cheesecloth).

In the past, foodstuffs were often strained through a fine cloth known as muslin or cheesecloth. Nowadays, this cloth is often replaced with a fine sieve.

Side Dishes

&

Vegetables

Artichoke Fricassee

La Varenne, Le Cuisinier françois, 1651

Simple, natural recipes like this one show to what extent the cuisine of the "Grand Century" aimed to highlight the "vray goust" (true taste) of produce.

SERVES 6

18 poivrade artichokes (small purple artichokes from Provence)
100 g/½ cup butter
2 cloves
1 Tbsp. lemon juice
a pinch of nutmeg
salt & pepper to taste

Pour a litre/quart of water with a bit of lemon juice into a large bowl. Snap off the artichoke stems and remove the outer leaves until there's no green left. Cut off the tips of the leaves and remove the choke (the hairy middle) by scraping at it with a knife or a spoon. Leave the artichoke hearts to soak in the lemon water for 15 minutes.

Drain them and cut them in quarters. Melt the butter in a heavy frying pan. Put the quartered artichokes in with the cloves; season with salt and pepper to taste. Cover and cook on medium heat until the vegetables are tender but still firm.

Squeeze some lemon juice over them and season with the nutmeg. Correct the seasoning before serving as a side dish with a fish stew.

Fried Artichokes

La Varenne, Le cuisinier françois, 1651

SERVES 6

6 poivrade or other purple
artichokes
100 g/ ⅔ cup flour
1 tsp. fine salt
100 g/½ cup butter
1 bunch flat-leaf parsley
3 Tbsp. oil

.Remove the outer leaves of the artichokes. Snap the stems off about an inch from the base and peel the stumps that remain. Remove the tips of the leaves and cut each artichoke into quarters. Blanch them in a large pot of boiling water for about 10 minutes.

Drain the pieces and dry them carefully with paper towels. Mix the flour and salt in a soup dish. Dredge the artichoke quarters in the flour mixture and shake off the excess. Melt the butter in a pan then sauté the artichokes, turning them over from time to time. Drain them on paper towels.

Wash, pat dry and roughly chop the parsley. Fry it quickly in a pan in very hot oil. Sprinkle it over the fried artichokes, grind a bit of pepper over them and serve immediately.

Asparagus in Cream

Coupez-les bien menues, et n'y laissez rien que le vert, fricassez-les avec beurre bien frais ou lard fondu, persil et ciboule, ou un bouquet, après cela, faites-les fort peu mitonner avec de la crème bien fraîche, et servez si vous voulez avec peu de muscade.

La Varenne, Le cuisinier françois, 1651

Asparagus, a herbaceous plant native to southern Europe but perfectly adapted to more northern regions, was all the rage in Versailles. To satisfy this demand, the King's kitchen garden had a large asparagus patch, which had chestnut-branch trellises to protect if from hungry rabbits. Only the green tips of asparagus were eaten at the King's table.

SERVES 6

1 kg (2 lb.) green, California-type asparagus

20 g/ 1½ Tbsp. butter

1 big shallot

2 cloves garlic

5 cl / ⅓ cup dry white wine or vegetable bouillon

20 cl / ⅘ cup light cream

a few sprigs flat-leaf parsley

1 small bunch fresh chives

1 pinch grated nutmeg

Choose the youngest, most slender asparagus you can find. Boil some water with a good pinch of coarse salt in a large pot. While the water's coming to the boil, peel and chop the shallot and onion. Wash the asparagus and snap off the hard ends, then slip the whole asparagus into the pot of boiling water. Let it come back to the boil, then blanche the asparagus for one minute. Remove them from the water immediately.

Rinse the asparagus in very cold water, and cut them into 3-cm./1- to 1½-inch lengths. Heat the butter in a large pan, being careful not to let it burn. Add the shallot and onion, and cook gently, without letting them brown. Then add the asparagus and season with the salt and pepper. Add the white wine or the bouillon. Cover and simmer over low heat for 10 minutes, stirring occasionally. Check if the asparagus is tender; add the garlic. Cook for 2 more minutes, then add the cream and a small knob of butter. Correct the seasoning if necessary. Top with the nutmeg and chives just before serving.

Our Tip

If you have the possibility, try to get wild asparagus in season. It's slender stems and strong taste are a delight. In France, it is extremely rare, but can sometimes be found at open-air markets in the South. Don't get taken in by the "pseudo-wild," a very thin type of asparagus that is omnipresent at Parisian market stalls in the month of May.

$\mathcal{A}$sparagus in Mild Sauce

Choisissez les plus grosses, ratissez-en les pieds et les lavez, puis les faites cuire dans de l'eau, les salez bien, et ne les laissez trop cuire ; étant cuites, mettez-les égoutter, et faites une sauce avec du beurre bien frais, peu de vinaigre, sel, muscade, et un jaune d'œuf pour lier la sauce, laquelle prenez garde qu'elle ne se tourne, et servez-les bien garnis de ce que vous voulez.

La Varenne, Le cuisinier françois, 1651

 This aptly named sauce is none other than our modern bechamel, or white sauce.

SERVES 6

2 kg/4 ½ lb. white asparagus

FOR THE SAUCE

40 g / 3 Tbsp. cup very fresh butter

1 egg yolk

25 to 30 l to 1¼ cup hot water

40 g/ ¼ cup flour

1 Tbsp. vinegar

1 pinch de nutmeg

In a large pot, boil water with a small handful of coarse salt. Use a vegetable peeler to carefully peel the asparagus, holding them by the tip. Wash them before putting them in the boiling water. Let them cook for about 20 minutes or so, until they are tender but still firm.

While the asparagus is cooking, prepare the sauce: melt the butter gently in a thick-bottomed saucepan. Sprinkle the flour into the melted butter. Stir this mixture and let it thicken before adding the hot water, as necessary, then season with salt and pepper to taste. Stir until the sauce thickens

Off the heat, add the egg yolk thinned with the vinegar, stirring continually. Finish with the pinch of nutmeg.

Drain the asparagus well before placing it in a large serving dish. Serve the sauce separately in a sauceboat. Each guest can thus add the amount of sauce that suits his or her taste.

Asparagus Ragout

La Varenne, Le cuisinier françois, 1651

SERVES 6

1 kg/2 lb. tender young green asparagus
50 g / ¼ butter
1 shallot
a few sprigs flat-leaf parsley
1 clove garlic
10 cl/ ⅓ cup poultry stock
salt & pepper to taste

Wash the asparagus and remove the hard ends. Blanch the asparagus whole in a large pot of boiling water for a few minutes. Drain and cut into 4-cm./1½- to 2-inch lengths. Melt the butter in a deep pan, add the chopped shallot and the crushed garlic.

Then add the asparagus, salt and pepper, and simmer over low heat for 30 minutes, shaking and stirring frequently. If need be, moisten with the chicken stock as it cooks. Sprinkle the finely chopped parsley over just before serving.

Mushroom Ragout

La Varenne, Le Cuisinier françois, 1651

Massialot said that cooking is "when things taste like what they are." For this very natural recipe, you can use any kind of mushrooms you like. A panful of chanterelle or boletus mushrooms makes a marvellous side dish for a roast duck, for example.

For 6, you'll need: 1 kg/2 lb. mushrooms, 100 g / ½ cup fresh butter, 1 bunch scallions, a few sprigs flat-leaf parsley, and possibly, ⅕ cup poultry bouillon, peel of ½ lemon.

The pairing of sweet and savoury, which is disappearing, was still seen in certain recipes from this time. The presence here of blancmange is a sign of this. At the time, blancmange was a sort of sweet almond jelly, which we propose replacing with 2 Tbsp. of s crème fraîche /sour cream, better adapted to contemporary tastes.

Stuffed Mushrooms

La Varenne, Le cuisinier françois, 1651

SERVES 6

18 big cultivated mushrooms

50 g de butter

100 g / ¼ pound veal

100 g / ¼ pound pork

1 shallot

1 clove garlic

2 Tbsp. olive oil

a few sprigs flat-leaf parsley

2 sprigs fresh thyme

1 small bunch chives

juice of 1 lemon

Preheat the oven (175 °C/350° F./Gas Mark ¾). Clean the mushrooms, remove the stems and scoop out a bit of the caps. Chop the meats, the shallot, the thyme and the parsley in the food processor. Add the olive oil before the salt and pepper.

Stuff the mushroom caps firmly with this mixture. Generously butter a baking dish large enough to allow you to place the stuffed caps in a single layer. Sprinkle a few bits of butter over the caps. Cover with aluminium foil and bake for 30 minutes.

Uncover and brown under the grill for a few minutes. Decorate with the chopped chives and squeeze the lemon juice over just before serving.

Cauliflower in White Butter

Pierre de Lune, Le Cuisinier, 1656

SERVES 6

1 cauliflower
1 clove
1 small knob butter

FOR THE WHITE-BUTTER SAUCE

100 g / ¼ lb. shallots
250 g / 1 cup fresh butter
10 cl / ½ cup dry white wine
5 cl / ¼ cup vinegar
1 pinch nutmeg
1 lemon
a few sprigs chervil
salt & white pepper to taste

Wash the cauliflower and separate it into florets. In a large pot, boil plenty of water with a handful of salt, the clove and the knob of butter. Carefully drop the cauliflower florets in, and let them boil until they are tender but still firm, approximately 15 minutes. Drain them carefully before arranging them in a single layer in a buttered baking dish that you should keep warm. Peel and finely chop the shallots.

Dice the butter and keep it in a dish filled with cold water. Pour the white wine and the vinegar into a large pot. Add the shallots and maintain them at a gentle boil until the shallots have gone transparent but there's still a bit of liquid left in the bottom of the pot. Then add 3 or 4 dice of butter and whisk gently. Continue in this manner until all of the butter has been incorporated. Then whip well, add salt and pepper to taste and top the cauliflower with your white butter sauce. Sprinkle with chopped chervil and a pinch of nutmeg. Decorate with a few slices of lemon with the skin and white pith removed.

*C*ucumber Fricassee with Fresh

La Varenne, Le cuisinier françois, 1651

SERVES 6

3 cucumbers
100 g/ ¼ lb. fresh butter
3 sprigs flat-leaf parsley
1 onion
salt & pepper to taste

Peel and thickly slice the cucumbers. Wash, pat dry and chop the parsley. In a deep frying pan, melt the chopped shallot in the melted butter.

After a few minutes, add the cucumber slices; season with salt and pepper and sprinkle over half the chopped parsley. Cook over medium heat for 20 minutes or until the vegetables are tender but still firm.

Before serving, drizzle a bit of olive oil over the cucumbers and top with the rest of the chopped parsley.

Spinach in Fresh Butter

La Varenne, Le Cuisinier françois, 1651

SERVES 6

2 kg / 4 ½ lb. spinach

100 g/ ¼ lb. fresh butter

1 onion

3 cloves

juice of ½ lemon

1 pinch nutmeg

salt & pepper to taste

FOR THE GARNISH

6 slices baguette

3 Tbsp. olive oil

1 clove garlic

1 lemon

salt & pepper to taste

Remove the stems from the spinach leaves and rinse them well, changing the water several times, and drain or spin them dry. Melt them gently in a large, covered pot, to which you have not added any butter or oil. Stir frequently to avoid sticking. When the spinach is cooked, drain off the excess liquid carefully, pressing it out with your hands if need be.

Melt the butter into the same pot, then put the spinach back in. Mix well, then add the onion stuck with the cloves, and the nutmeg. Season with the salt and pepper, and let it simmer at low heat for 15 minutes, stirring frequently. While the spinach is reducing, prepare your garnish. Peel the garlic and cut it in two. Rub the slices of bread with the garlic pieces. Moisten with the olive oil, season with the salt and pepper and brown in the oven.

For the lemon juice over the spinach and serve surrounded with the garlic toast and slices of lemon with the peel and white pith removed.

Green Peas Cooked in Lard

Faites fondre du lart et passez vos pois à la poësle ou dans un plat ou terrine, mettez sur le feu avec un paquet d'assaisonnement, un peu de sel, et y mettez un peu de bouillon, ne les couvrez point, ayez soin de les remuer souvent à petits feux, et les conservez les plus verts que vous pouvez, en servans mettez un peu de beurre frais et les remuez.

Pierre de Lune, Le Cuisinier, 1656

 In 1696, Madame de Maintenon wrote: "The green pea chapter is endless: expressions of impatience to be eating them, pleasure of having eaten them or joy at the expectation of eating them again soon are all I have heard hear for the past few days. There are ladies who, once they have dined with the King, and dined well at that, keep peas in their room to nibble on before retiring."

SERVES 6

3 kg / 6½ lb. unshelled peas

100 g / ¼ lb lard

1 bouquet garni (thyme, parsley, bay leaf)

20 cl / 1 cup vegetable bouillon

1 large knob butter

10 small white onions (optional)

salt & pepper to taste

Shell the peas. Melt the lard in a deep pan before adding the whole white onions, if you choose to include them. Add the peas, stir well to coat them with the fat, then pour the bouillon in. Finally, add the bouquet garni and simmer over low heat, stirring frequently.

When the peas are tenders, turn off the heat, remove the bouquet garni and add a large knob of fresh butter. Adjust the seasoning as required. Serve hot as a side dish with meat or fish.

Pumpkin Soup with Butter

SERVES 6

1.5 kg / 3 ½ lb pumpkin
150 g/ 1-⅓ cups butter
20 cl. / ⅘ cup water
1 medium onion
3 cloves
3 egg yolks (optional)
10 cl/ ½ cup chicken bouillon

Scoop out the pumpkin seeds and separate the flesh from the rind, then chop the flesh into chunks approximately 2 inches on all sides. Cook them in lightly salted water for 30 minutes. Drain them, then sauté them and the onion stuck with the cloves in butter in a deep pan. Season with salt and pepper as needed. Simmer over low heat for 30 minutes more.

If desired, add the egg yolks, thinned with the bouillon just before serving. You can serve this soup with slices of farmhouse bread drizzled with a bit of olive oil and toasted in the oven.

Pumpkin Soup with Milk

Pierre de Lune, Le cuisinier, 1656

SERVES 6

1 kg 500 / 3 ½ lb pumpkin
1 litre/1 quart milk
100 g / ¼ lb. fresh butter
1 bouquet garni (thyme, parsley, bay leaf)
a few sprigs flat-leaf parsley
1 small bunch fresh chives
a few sprigs fresh chervil
salt

FOR THE SOUP BOWL
5 thin slices farmhouse bread

Take a nice slab of pumpkin, remove the rind and scrape off the seeds. Cut the flesh into small chunks, and sauté them in a pot with the butter. Add salt and the bouquet garni and cook over low heat for an hour. Pour the warmed milk into the pot along with half of the chopped herbs. Cook for a few minutes more over high heat, stirring constantly.

Adjust the seasoning as necessary. Fry thin slices of farmhouse bread in butter, or toast them under the grill. Line the bottom of a soup bowl with 2 slices of fried or toasted bread, ladle the soup over them, and top with the rest of the chopped herbs.

Serve immediately with the remaining toast slices cut in half.

Our Tip

The success of this recipe depends on the quality of the ingredients. Choose a nice, freshly cut (slice of) pumpkin, with a bright colour, and make sure the butter and milk you use are top quality too.

Onion Ramekin

La Varenne, Le cuisinier françois, 1651

Might this be the ancestor of onion pizza?

SERVES 6

1 bunch green onions

1 small round loaf
farmhouse bread or a day-
old baguette

2 anchovy filets

1 clove garlic

25 g/ 2 Tbsp. butter

2 Tbsp. olive oil

salt & pepper to taste

Clean the onions, setting aside the youngest, most tender green stems. Roughly chop the white part of the onions in the blender or spice mixer. Melt the butter in a deep pan, add the onions and the rinsed and chopped anchovies. Cook on fairly high heat for 5 minutes, stirring frequently.

While the onions are cooking, slice the bread into fairly thin slices and rub them on both sides with the garlic, which you should first peel and crush lightly with a knife blade.

Place the slices on a baking sheet, drizzle a bit of olive oil over them and salt and pepper them lightly. Toast them in the oven for 2 minutes. Remove the slices and turn them over. Spread the onion-anchovy paste onto the untoasted side of the slices of bread. Drizzle a bit more olive oil on top, sprinkle on some pepper and put them under a very hot grill for 5 minutes, or until the onions begin to brown nicely.

Decorate your serving dish with the young green stems and serve immediately.

Desserts, Sweets

&

Drinks

*F*ashionable "Aumelette"

La Varenne, Le Pastissier françois, 1653

10 eggs

50 g/ ¼ cup butter

50 g/ ¼ cup currants (raisins)

50 g / 3/8 cup pine nuts

50 g/ ¼ cup caster sugar (granulated sugar)

5 cl / ¼ cup light cream

50 g/ ¼ cup candied lemon peel

1 tsp. rosewater

1 pinch salt

icing sugar

Put the currants (raisins) in a small bowl and soak them in hot water for 30 minutes. Break the eggs into a larger bowl, add the 50 g/ ¼ cup of sugar, the cream and the salt. Beat them well with a wire whisk or an electric beater. Add the drained, soaked currants and the candied lemon peel, diced as finely as possible. Melt the butter in a large frying pan and brown the pine nuts.

As soon as the nuts are brown (be careful not to let them burn), pour the beaten eggs into the pan and cook at very low heat for at least 45 minutes, or until the mixture is thoroughly cooked.

Just before serving, moisten the omelette with the rosewater and sprinkle generously with the icing sugar.

The Queen's Biscuits

Faites de la paste comme au chapitre precedent, sinon que vous y mettez moins d'œuf, car il faut que la paste du biscuit à la Reyne soit un peu plus ferme : c'est pourquoi au lieu par exemple de huict œufs ce sera assez d'en mettre six. Lors que la paste sera preste, vous la coucherez avec une gâche sur du papier bien blanc, et vous ferez ces biscuits ronds comme des petits pains, et on les poudrera par dessus avec du sucre. Il faut donner l'âtre un peu plus chaud au biscuit à la Reyne, qu'au biscuit commun. Aussi-tost que le biscuit à la Reyne sera cuit, vous le tirerez hors du four, et le detacheres hors du dessus son papier, en coulant asdroitement un cousteau mince entre le biscuit et le papier. La pâte " biscuit commun " : " Cassés par exemple huict œufs dans une escuelle, battez les comme si c'estoit pour faire une omelette ; adjoustez pour environ deux liards de coriandre battuë, ou d'anis vert, et une livre de sucre en poudre, delayez un peu ces choses ensemble, puis y adjouster trois bons quarterons ou pres d'une livre de fleur de farine ; il faut delayer ensemble toutes ces choses exactement, et les battre jusques à ce que la paste devienne blanche, et le biscuit sera d'autant plus beau et mieux fait que la paste aura esté battuë…

La Varenne, Le Pastissier françois, 1653

MAKES APPROXIMATELY 40 BISCUITS

3 eggs

200 g/1 cup sugar + 50 g/ ¼ cup

250 g/ 2 cups flour

1 tsp. powdered green anise

Preheat the oven to 190°C/375° F./Gas Mark 5. In a large bowl, beat the eggs well, and add the 200 g/1 cup of sugar and the anise. Use an electric beater to whip the mixture until it tuns pale and has doubled in size. Sift the flour and add it little by little to the beaten eggs. Let the batter sit for 20 minutes. Cover the baking sheet with baking paper. Drop teaspoonfuls of batter onto the baking sheet, shaping them into "little biscuits as round as buns."

Sprinkle each biscuit lightly with the extra 50 g/ ¼ cup of sugar before baking for about 10 minutes. Remove them from the hot plaque as soon as they are out of the oven and eat them warm or cooled to room temperature.

If you prefer to keep them for a later date, let them cool completely before storing them in an airtight metal biscuit tin.

Applesauce à la Dauphine

Apples were among the most frequently eaten fruits in the 17th century. Although applesauce was also a well-known preparation, the recipe proposed by Massialot in Nouvelle Instruction pour les confitures ("New Instructions for Jams"), has a touch of distinction, thanks to its uniquely refined presentation. Choose a stewing apple that doesn't soften too quickly, like Jonagoreds. For the red colouring, forget about the insect-based dye called "cochenille" that Massialot suggests, and prefer modern food colouring or some puréed raspberries.

SERVES 6

1.3 kg/3 lb. apples
75 g/ ⅜ cup sugar
juice of a half a lemon
red food colouring

Peel, quarter and core the apples. Leave 2 of them in quarters. For the others, use a melon-ball scoop to cut out little balls ("like plums"), that you should drizzle some lemon juice over to keep from browning. Put the leftover bits of apple as well as the two quartered ones in a small saucepan with the sugar, and cook over low heat. Keep an eye on the mixture as it cooks, and add a bit of water (or apple juice) if it starts to stick.

After about 20 minutes or cooking, mash the apples into sauce and put the sauce back on the stove for 10 minutes, adding the little apple balls. Cook until the balls are just tender.

Turn your sauce a lovely shade of pink with a few drops of food colouring or spoonfuls of raspberry purée. Refrigerate and serve cold.

 Baked Stuffed Apples

SERVES 6

6 apples

1 orange

1 jar of apricot jam

50 g/ ⅜ cup slivered almonds

10 cl/ ½ cup mellow white wine (e.g. Monbazillac)

icing sugar

Preheat the oven (175°C/350° F./ Gas Mark 3/4). Wash the whole apples carefully. Scoop out the core with an apple corer or the tip of a vegetable peeler. It doesn't matter if the hole is fairly wide. Peel the orange well so that there's no white pith attached, and roughly chop the flesh.

Fill each apple with first the apricot jam, then a few bits of orange, the slivered almonds and finally a bit more jam. Butter a baking dish well, arrange the stuffed apples in it, moisten with the white wine and cover with a sheet of aluminium foil.

Bake for 50 minutes at 160°C/310° F./Gas Mark 2/3. Sprinkle with icing sugar before serving, or follow Massialot's advice and, "Serve them in a bit of syrup as some people do."

Cotignac d'Orléans

*C'est celui qui a le plus de réputation, comme parmi les noix blanches celles de Rouen.
En voici la matière:*

*Prenez vos coings et coupez-les par morceaux, que vous pèlerez et nettoierez de leurs
pépins. Ayez en même temps 2 livres de sucre cuit à passer pour 6 livres de fruits; et
ayant mis les coings, faites cuire le tout ensemble pour les mettre en pâte; vous les
passerez ensuite dans une toile neuve pour les pouvoir bien presser et ce qui sera sorti
vous servira pour votre cotignac.*

*Faites cuire à cet effet encore 4 livres de sucre à perlé, puis vous y mettrez le jus et
quand tout sera revenu à la même cuisson vous le descendrez de dessus le feu et vous le
mettrez dans vos boîtes ou autres pots que vous laisserez à l'air quelques jours avant
que de les couvrir.*

Massialot, Nouvelle Instruction pour les confitures, 1692

 Cotignac – from the Provençal name coudougnat, meaning "quince" – designates quince or orange jelly. For this lovely golden jelly, Massialot recommends the Orleans quince, "the one with the best reputation, like Rouen's white walnuts"

*FOR APPROXIMATELY 1.2 KG /
2 ½ LB. OF COTIGNAC*

*1 kg/2 ¼ lb. quince
700 à 800 g/ 3½ to 4 cups
caster (granulated) sugar*

Wash the quince and wipe them to remove the fine down, quarter them, and remove the hard centres and the pits, which you should tie into a bit of muslin (cheesecloth). Put the quince and the knot of muslin in a large pot, and cover them with cold water. Cook until the flesh goes soft, drain and throw away the knot. Press the quince through a sieve to get as much juice as possible, but without crushing the fruit to the extent that it clouds the juice.

Weigh the juice, pour it into a copper jam pan, and add the same weight of sugar. Bring to the boil and cook over low heat for about 15 minutes. Stop cooking when a drop of jelly on a chilled plate sets quickly.

Skim any scum from the surface and pour quickly into jam jars that have been boiled, and close immediately. Turn the sealed jam jars over immediately and leave upside down overnight.

Pistachio Custard

Massialot, Le cuisinier roïal et bourgeois, 1691

SERVES 6

150 g/ shelled, unsalted pistachio nuts
1 piece candied lemon peel
1 lime
1 Tbsp. flour
4 egg yolks
100 g/ ½ cup sugar
50 cl/1 pint milk

FOR THE MERINGUE

6 egg whites
100 g/ ½ cup sugar

Toast the pistachio nuts briefly in a very hot, dry pan, before blending them in a food processor. With a vegetable peeler, peel off the zest of the lime without taking the white pith. Add it and the candied lemon peel to the food processor.

Stir the egg yolks and the flour together in a large bowl. Add the sugar and mix well. Gradually add the milk, stirring constantly. Add the powdered pistachios. Strain everything through a sieve. If need be, strain it several times until you are left with a smooth cream that you will cook for a few minutes. When it's cooked, pour it into a serving dish and chill before serving.

If you prefer to serve it hot, make a meringue: beat the egg whites until they form stiff peaks. Add the sugar gradually. Put the cream in a baking dish, spread the meringue on top and warm it in the oven until the top begins to brown, about 2 minutes.

Custard known as Friend's Pie

Battez 2 ou 3 jaunes d'œufs avec une poignée de sucre en poudre, et quand ils seront bien délayés, versez-les dans une abaisse ou croûte dressée pour faire la tarte. Étendez-y ce premier appareil, puis vous mettrez par-dessus autant qu'il sera besoin de la farce au fromage. La tarte étant garnie suffisamment faites-la cuire; et lorsqu'elle sera presque cuite, poudrez-la de sucre et l'arrosez un peu d'eau de rose; remettez-la au four pour achever de la faire cuire et pour faire glacer le sucre.

Pour la farce au fromage, prenez gros comme 2 coings de fromage mou non écrémé, la grosseur d'une ou deux noix de fromage sec un peu affiné qui soit broyé ou râpé ou seulement coupé en morceaux bien petits, du sel à la discrétion et environ un quarteron de bon beurre non salé qui soit fondu; ajoutez-y le blanc et le jaune d'un ou 2 œufs, mêlez ensemble toutes ces choses et les manier bien pour les délier et y ajoutez un peu d'eau froide si l'appareil est trop épais. Il faut aussi y ajouter environ la grosseur d'un œuf de farine ou de pain blanc.

La Varenne, Le Pastissier françois, 1653

Thanks to this cheerfully named dessert, La Varenne would seem to be the ancestor of our modern pastry chefs specialised in cheesecakes.

SERVES 6

300 g/ ⅔ lb. short-crust (pie crust) dough

400 g/ 1 lb. cottage cheese

10 cl/ ½ cup crème fraîche (sour cream)

1 Saint Marcellin cheese

50 g/ ½ cup butter

80 g + 1 Tbsp./ ⅜ cup + 1 Tbsp. sugar

2 whole eggs + 2 yolks

30 g/ ¼ cup flour

Roll the pie-crust dough out on a floured work surface. Make it big enough to line a large, flat, buttered pie dish. Beat two egg yolks with a spoonful of sugar and brush this mix onto the pie crust.

To prepare the custard filling, first mix the sugar with the just barely melted butter. Then stir in the cottage cheese, the crème fraîche (sour cream) and the Saint Marcellin, which you will have mashed, chopped or grated, depending on its texture. Mix everything well. Add two whole eggs and beat well. Sprinkle the flour over the egg mixture, stir it in to avoid lumps. Pour the mixture into the pie crust and bake for 40 to 45 minutes, at 180 ° C/350° F./Gas Mark 4. The top should be nicely browned. If you wish, in La Varenne's footsteps, when the tart "is almost cooked, sprinkle it with sugar and a few drops of rose-water; put it back in the oven to finish baking and to glaze the sugar." Serve well chilled.

Our Tips

Adding the juice of a half a lemon just before cooking gives a nice tart touch to this fine dessert.

If you prefer a slightly milder, creamier custard, replace the cottage cheese with 500 g/1 lb. drained 'fromage blanc en faisselle'.

How to Make "Macarons"

Pilez des amandes, ainsi qu'il à esté proposé au chapitre du masse-pain, puis vous les pilerez et reduirez en paste très douce : par exemple une livre adjoustez y auatnt pesant de sucre en poudre et quatre blancs d'œufs : meslez ces choses nesemble en y adjoustant un peu d'eau rose, et les rebattez derechef dans le mortier pour faire cette paste bien lainte, il faut pourtant qu'elle soit un peu mollette. Quand cette paste sera preste, couchez la sur du papier blanc éloignez quelque peu l'un de l'autre, et que ces morceaux soient un peu longs en forme de macaron, et les poudrez par-dessus de sucre fin : puis on les mettra au four pour secher jusques à ce qu'ils soient bien fermes par dessus en les touchant. Il faut que la chaleur du four soit douce comme au chapitre du masse-pain, et que l'âtre soit pourtant un peu chaud afin de pousser la paste, et la faire bouffer…

La Varenne, Le Pastissier françois, 1653

Certain regions and cities in France are famous for their 'macarons' (not to be confused with macaroons, these are almond meringues, nowadays often served filled with jam or a chocolate ganache). In the city of Nancy, "commercial" production of macarons dates back to the 17th century. Carmelite nuns made them popular, as they followed St. Theresa of Avila's advice: "Almonds are good for girls who don't eat meat." During the Revolution, two nuns who lived in the town specialised in making this treat. They were nicknamed the Sœurs Macaron (the "Macaron Sisters"), and a street in town still bears their name.

FOR APPROXIMATELY 30 MACARONS

4 egg whites

250 g/ 1¼ cups fine sugar

250 g/ 1 ¾ cups powdered almonds

1 pinch salt

rose water, powdered cocoa, pure vanilla extract (optional)

Cover a baking sheet with a sheet of baking paper. In one large bowl, mix the powdered almonds and the sugar. In a second large bowl, beat the egg whites (with a pinch of salt) into stiff peaks. Gently fold the egg whites into the first bowl; now is the time to add one of the flavourings if you choose to do so. Using a pastry tube or a spoon, drop spoonfuls of this meringue mixture onto the baking paper; don't put them too close together, as they will puff up during cooking.

Bake for 15 minutes at 180 ° C/350° F./Gas Mark 4 in the centre of the over – too low, and the tops will brown. Check on your macarons regularly, as ovens vary, and your macarons might cook more quickly. One rule: they must be removed form the oven white they are still ivory white, like meringues. As soon as you have removed them from the oven, use a spatula to take them off the baking sheet and let them cool on a cutting board or a plate. Sealed in an airtight biscuit tin they can be kept "fresh" for up to 3 weeks.

Eggs à l'anglaise (Eggs English Style)

Prenez une douzaine et demi d'œufs, avec des prunes, des brugnoles, de l'écorce de citron confites et coupées en morceaux, des raisins de Corinthe, des macarons pilés et 2 pots de crème. Mêlez bien le tout ensemble et assaisonnez-le de sel, de cannelle et de sucre; cela fait mettez-le dans une tourtière avec du beurre affiné et faites-le cuire à petit feu. Lorsque vos œufs seront cuits, glacez-les avec un peu d'eau de senteur et de sucre musqué, sans les garnir aucunement de quoi que ce soit.

L'Escole parfaite des Officiers de bouche, 1662

For this recipe, the original author used brugnoles, a small, round fruit that has practically disappeared today, but which can be replaced with cherries. This is probably the ancestor of a popular French pudding called 'clafoutis'!

SERVES 6

10 eggs
500 g/ 1 lb. cherries
50 g/ ¼ cup sugar
20 cl/1 cup crème fraîche (sour cream)
25 g/ ⅛ cup candied orange peel
1 untreated lemon
4 small, unflavoured macarons or meringues
50 g/ ¼ cup raisins
50 g/ ¼ cup butter
1 pinch powdered cinnamon
1 Tbsp. orange-blossom water
icing sugar
a pinch of salt

Break the eggs into a large bowl. Add the sugar, cream and salt. Beat well with a hand or electric beater. Dice the orange peel very fine and grate the lemon peel. Add them to the beaten eggs, along with the crushed macarons or meringues. Whisk everything. Add the raisins and the washed, whole cherries. (Remove the stems but leave the stones (pits). Melt the butter in a pan and add the omelette preparation. Let it cook over very low heat for at least an hour, or until it is completely cooked through. Just before serving, moisten with the orange-blossom water and sprinkle with icing sugar.

Our Tip

This dessert can be eaten warm but is particularly tasty cold. You can make it several hours ahead of time and keep it in the refrigerator. Take it out 30 minutes before you sit down, and sprinkle the icing sugar on just before serving.

*E*ggs à l'hypocras

Pierre de Lune, Le Cuisinier, 1656

Louis XIV is famous for having been wild about hard-boiled eggs served all different ways. People's palates at the time were accustomed to combinations that we would find odd today: 'œufs à l'hypocras', hard-boiled egg fritters served with delicately flavoured mulled-wine syrup, is a case in point. But try it, you may be pleasantly surprised!

SERVES 6

6 hard-boiled eggs

FOR THE FRITTER BATTER

80 g / ½ cup flour

3 egg yolks

10 cl/ ½ cup wine (Bordeaux rosé)

2 pinches powdered cinnamon

40 g/ ⅓ cup butter

FOR THE CARAMEL

20 cl/ 1 cup rosé wine

100 g/ ½ cup sugar

3 cloves

a few drops vinegar

FOR THE PRESENTATION

2 pinches powdered cinnamon

a few pomegranate seeds (optional)

Cut the boiled eggs in two. Make the fritter batter by carefully adding the wine to the flour and then stirring in the beaten egg yolks. Heat the butter in a pan, dip the halved egg in the batter and fry them, being careful not to let the batter burn.

Arrange the egg fritters m in a pyramid on a serving dish.

Dissolve the sugar into the wine over low heat, add the cloves and a few drops of vinegar. Simmer this mulled wine, keeping a careful eye on it, until it has reduced to a somewhat thick syrup.

Pour this lovely pink syrup over the pyramid of eggs.

Hypocras

We suggest using a Bordeaux rosé for 'eggs à l'hypocras', but in Le Cuisinier françois, La Varenne gives this recipe for a lightly spiced drink.

'In a large earthenware recipient, mix 2 quarts of good white wine (try Chablis), 1 pound sugar, 30 g/1 oz./ 4 ½ tablespoons cinnamon, 2 white peppercorns, 1 lemon cut into pieces and let everything steep for a few hours. Put some sugar pounded with a tiny grain of musk into a small cloth bag. Place this instrument in a cloth funnel, and pour your steeped wine through it. Add a glass of milk. Stir well and taste.'

$\mathcal{R}$aspberry Soup

Pierre de Lune, Le Cuisinier, 1656

This recipe has evolved in interesting ways over the centuries. Nowadays, in summer, more and more restaurants serve a variety of fresh-fruit soups, often with ice cream, sherbet or home-made biscuits. Even today, innovative young chefs take inspiration from this "potage" dreamt up Pierre de Lune in the 17th century to produce an elegant but inexpensive dessert.

SERVES 6

400 g/ 1 lb. raspberries

25 cl/ cup water

25 cl/1 cup mellow white wine

100 g/ ½ cup sugar

1 cinnamon stick

6 small, unflavoured 'macarons' or meringues

fresh mint leaves (optional) as garnish

Bring the water and wine to the boil with the cinnamon stick and the sugar. Once it has boiled, lower the heat and let it simmer for an hour. When this syrup has cooled completely – at least an hour before serving – add the raspberries.

Place a small 'macaron' or meringue in each coupe, then ladle some "soup" over each macaron. Top with a mint leaf for garnish.

Our Tip

If you follow Pierre de Lune's recipe to the letter, you'll get a sweet raspberry 'coulis' (sauce) that makes a delicious accompaniment to Monsieur de La Varenne's "Custard Known as Friend's Pie".

To Make Jellied Applesauce

There was a profusion of apples in the King's Orchard. La Quintinie worked at acclimatising a great number of varieties in order to select only the best for the King's table. The "reinette" (little queen) was one of his favourites, as you can see in his own words:
"Among the apples that are good for eating, whether raw or cooked, I count seven main varieties: Reinette grise, Reinette blanche, Calville d'automne, Fenouillet, Courspendu, Api, Violette. There are others that I wouldn't shout about, although they really aren't bad. They are Rambour, Calville d'été, Consinotte, Orgeran, Jérusalem, Pommes de glace, Francatu, Haute Bonté, Royauté, Ronvezeau, Châtaignier, Pigeonet, etc." (Instructions for gardens, t. I, Part 3, ch. IV).
Audiger's simple but elegant recipe, in La Maison réglée ("The Well-Run Household"), highlights apple's delicate flavour.

SERVES 6

9 "reine de reinette" apples (approximately 1.5 kg/3 ½ lb.)

375 g/ ¾ lb. sugar

Quarter 6 apples, peel and core them, setting the skins aside; place the fruit in a large bowl of cold water to keep them from browning. Wash and quarter the last 3 apples. Put them in a large saucepan with the skins set aside from the other apples and 1.5 litres (1 ½ qt.) of water. Bring it to a boil, then gently boil for 30 minutes. Filter the juice through a fine sieve or some muslin and put it back on the heat, with the sugar. Poach the apple quarters for about 10 minutes, making sure that they are cooked, but still firm.

Then follow Audiger's recommendations: "When they are cooked, you will remove the pan from the heat. You will take them out one by one and will press them very gently between two spoons to expel the juice, then arrange them on a dish."

While you are dealing with the quartered apples, keep cooking the syrup, keeping an eye on it to make sure it doesn't burn. After about 50-60 minutes, turn off the heat, let the jelly set lightly, then decorate the top with the quartered apples "which can be kept thus for four or five days."

$\mathcal{P}$ear-Meat Pie

Pears were one of the favourite fruits in Louis XIV's court. The King's Gardener took good of them and made sure that they were served ripe to perfection.
This confection, a harmonious blend of pears, raisins, pine nuts and candied lemon, has a very modern flavour.

SERVES 6

375 g/ ¾ lb. pie crust dough
1½ kg/ 3½ lb. pears
150g/ ¾ cup sugar
30 g/ ¼ cup pine nuts
60 g/ ⅜ cup raisins
1 untreated lemon
4 pinches powdered cinnamon

"Excellent Pears":
Cuisse-Madame
Muscat-Fle
Doyenné
Franc-réal
Pastourelle
La Vilaine d'Anjou

"Good Pears":
La Bergamotte
La Virgoulé
Poire à la Reine
Pucelle de Flandre
La Blanquette
Satin-Vert
La Non-Commune des Défuntes
La Fondante de Brest

"Mediocre Pears":
Poires de Monsieur
L'Angleterre
Le Chat-Brûlé
La Musette
La Crapaudine
Le Sucrin noir
La Poire de Jasmin
La Frangipane
L'Or d'Automne
Le Sans-nom de Monsieur Le Jeune (…)"

La Quintinie, Instructions for Gardens, t. I, Part 3.

On a floured work surface, roll out the dough in two parts: the first one to line the bottom of a deep-dish pie pan, the other to make a top crust.

Prepare the filling. Soak the raisins in warm water. Wash and brush the lemon, then peel it, taking care to get it as thin as possible, and not to have any of the bitter white pith under the zest. Cut the zest into tiny pieces and boil them twice. Drain them and candy them in a light syrup that you can make in a small saucepan with 50 g/ ¼ cup of sugar and 10 cl/ ½ cup of water. Simmer gently for about 10 minutes until you get a still-runny syrup with the lemon peel. While the lemon is simmering, peel the pears and cut them into bite-size pieces. Combine the pears, pine nuts, drained raisins, candied lemon peel, the rest of the sugar and the cinnamon in a large bowl. Mix well and let it sit for 15 minutes.

Preheat the oven to 200°C/425° F./Gas Mark 7. Pour the pear mixture into the bottom half of the piecrust and cover with the top crust, sealing the edges well and brushing the top with an egg yolk thinned with a tablespoon of water. Cut a "chimney" into the top crust, which you can keep open with a small cardboard tube.

Bake for 1 hour. Keep an eye on it as its cooking: when the top is nicely browned, you can cover it lightly with aluminium foil to keep it from burning. Let it cool slightly before serving warm, or cool and then chill to serve cold.

Our Tip

Pears tend to expel a lot of juice during baking. Be careful to buy pears that are firm and not too juicy. The variety will depend on the season, but in our experience, Conference pears are excellent in this recipe. And just for the pleasure, it's worth looking up the pear inventory La Quintinie established: he cited a total of 500 varieties!

$\mathcal{A}$pple Cream Pie

L'Escole parfaite des Officiers de bouche, 1662

This recipe, from L'Escole parfaite des Officiers de bouche ("The Perfect School of Officers of the King's Table") was made with applesauce made from "rainette" apples, an old-fashioned tart, juicy variety of apples with skin that was lightly spotted, rather like small frogs' skin. In autumn in France, one can still sometimes find reinettes du Mans or reinettes clochard ; if you can't find them, try chantecler apples, which are quite similar to reinettes, or any other tart cooking apple.

SERVES 6

500 g/1 lb. puff (flaky, croissant-type) pastry dough

1.5 kg/ 3½ lb. rainette or other tart cooking apples

20 cl/1 cup monbazillac wine

100 g/ ½ cup sugar

3 pinches cinnnamon

2 Tbsp. orange-blossom water

1 egg yolk

** Muslin cloth, originally made of horsehair, silk or thread, was long used to sieve or filter culinary preparations.*

Prepare the vol-au-vent pastry case: on a floured board, roll out the dough to about 2-cm/ ¾-inch thick and cut out a 25-cm-/10-inch-wide circle. Brush it with the egg yolk thinned with a teaspoonful of water. With the tip of a knife, make light incisions around the edge of the circle. For the top crust, again with the tip of the knife, lightly trace a second circle (without cutting all the way through the dough), 3 cm/one inch inside the first. Draw a trellis pattern on the top crust. Place the dough on a buttered baking tray and bake in the oven (200° C/400° F./Gas Mark 6) for half an hour to 35 minutes. The top should be nicely browned. Take it out of the oven, carefully remove the top crust, and scrape out and throw away any white, doughy bits clogging the inside of the case. Let it cool.

For the filling, peel the apples, put them in a saucepan with the monbazillac and cook gently, uncovered, over low heat for an hour. Off the heat, add the sugar, cinnamon and orange-blossom water; blend well to obtain a smooth "creamy" applesauce.

When the applesauce has cooled, fill the vol-au-vent case and chill it in the refrigerator. Serve cold.

*M*elon Marmalade Pie

Pierre de Lune, Le Cuisinier, 1656

SERVES 6

250 g/ ½ lb. puff (flaky, croissant-type) pie-crust dough

1.7 to 2 kg/4 to 5 lbs. ripe whole melon

(2 melons, which should give about 2¼ lb melon flesh)

10 cl/ ½ cup Monbazillac (sweet white wine)

120 g/ ¼ lb. unflavoured 'macarons' or meringues

100 g/ ¼ lb. sugar

3 pinches powdered cinnamon

icing sugar and 1 tsp. orange-blossom water for serving

Preheat the oven to 180°C/350° F./Gas Mark 4. Peel and seed the melons. Cut the flesh into chunks and put them in a saucepan with the Monbazillac. Bring to the boil and simmer, uncovered. Keep an eye on the melon as it cooks, and cover if the juice is evaporating too quickly.

While the melon marmalade is cooking, roll the dough out to line a buttered pie plate, then cover the bottom with aluminium foil and dried beans (or marbles) and bake blind for about 20 minutes.

When the marmalade is just right (count 35 to 40 minutes), add the crumbled macarons, sugar and cinnamon and stir well. Remove the aluminium foil and the beans from the pie crust. Pour in the melon marmalade in and put the pie back in the oven for another 15 minutes. Chill and serve sprinkled with icing sugar and a few drops of orange-blossom water.

Wine of the Gods

SERVES 6

1 bottle very good
Burgundy

500 g/ 1 lb. "reinette" (or
any tart cooking) apples

300 g/ ⅔ lb. lemons

75 g/ ⅜ cup brown sugar

Peel and core the whole apples, then slice them into rings. Peel the lemons carefully, so that no white pith remains, and slice them as well. In a large bowl, top a layer of apple rings with a layer of lemon slices, then sprinkle the lemon with sugar. Continue in this way until you have used up all of the fruit and sugar.

Pour the wine over the fruit, and cover the bowl with plastic wrap. Let it sit for at least 2 hours before removing the fruit. Strain the wine through muslin and pour it into a pitcher and keep cool until serving as a cocktail or before dinner.

Contents

ISBN : 978-2-911665-98-1
© Archives & Culture, 26 bis rue Paul Barruel, 75015 Paris

Achevé d'imprimer 1ᵉʳ trimestre 2016 en Espagne
Conception maquette : Martine Fichter

Crédit photographique : Couverture : © J.F. Rivière/Top